Healing *after* Divorce...

IT'S ABOUT TIME!

Healing *after* Divorce...

IT'S ABOUT TIME!

Joanne F. Lyons, M.Ed.

Copyright 2008

© *2008 Joanne Fields Lyons*
Third printing 2010

1st printing 2008 and 2nd printing 2009 under different title, "It's About Time! It's ALL About Time…time, love, and tenderness."

All rights reserved. No part of this book may be reproduced or transmitted in any form or by any means, electronic or mechanical, including photocopying, recording, or by any information storage and retrieval system, without written permission from the author, except for the inclusion of brief quotations in a review.

Precautionary Advice

This book is for informational purposes and for encouragement. If you are having feelings of ending it all, seek professional psychiatric help. If you find you just can't go through this ordeal alone, find support groups and/or a psychologist to assist you through this time in your life. Do not be afraid to seek professional help. They are there to help you.

The case studies in this book are based on real life experiences. Names have been changed. Events have been condensed and/or compiled from several different individuals' experiences, to assist in the relativity of the topic. Any similarities to any one individual are coincidental.

Dedication

I dedicate this book to all those that are going through or have gone through a difficult separation and divorce. I want you to know that you are not alone. God is always with you. He is a huge resource as well as therapists, support groups, books, self-guided workbooks, web sites and individuals that you meet who have experienced what you are experiencing and have experienced.

Acknowledgement and Thanks

I thank God for always being there and for all of my life's experiences. I thank my parents, Virginia F. Bradley and John R. Fields, for raising me with a faith in God and encouraging me to do my best. I thank my husband, Tom O'Brien, for renewing my confidence in my God-given abilities and encouraging me to follow the Holy Spirit's leading. I acknowledge my son, Andrew Lyons, for his steady and consistent emotional strength. I thank Sharon Pollack Nowell for her keen eye and editing skills. I acknowledge the ministry team and the ladies of Oasis for their dedication and fortitude. And last but not least, I thank Annie Kelley Cox for her undying faith in the ministry and constant encouragement and support.

CONTENTS

Preface   3
Introduction   5

PART I
Time

Chapter One *Healing*   9
It is going to take time, love, and tenderness. You have a unique opportunity.

Chapter Two *Hurt Over Time*   27
Types of emotional scarring (abuse) occurring over a lifetime.

Chapter Three *Healing Takes Time*   47
Building a self-esteem structure. The components are love, patience, positive awareness, centeredness, belief, tenderness, and self-talk.

Chapter Four *Give It Time*   65
Being complete and whole as God made you. A spouse is a complement.

Chapter Five *Take the Time*   83
Healing from the inside out. The inner child and taking responsibility of re-parenting the *self*.

Chapter Six *Take A Long Time*   101
Taking long clear looks at the marriage, reconciliation and/or moving on.

Chapter Seven *Take A Really Long Time*   117
Stages of Loss, related to separation/divorce: Denial, Anger, Bargaining, Grief or Depression, and Acceptance.

PART II
Love

Chapter Eight *Love of Self*   133
Evaluate self-words related to love of self.

Chapter Nine *Love of Friends*   153
Analyze how to love others.

Chapter Ten *Love of Dating*   **165**
Cautions regarding places, persons and returning to dating.

Chapter Eleven *Love of Marriage*   **187**
The relationship of marriage is not all romantic and glamorous. Developing good and essential communication before marriage.

PART III
Tenderness

Chapter Twelve *Showing Tenderness to Yourself and Others*   **203**
Showing love in a truly loving way. Tenderness is giving love that flows out of us and doesn't drain us. Recharging the Love batteries.

Epilogue   221
Afterword   222

Preface

Maybe some of your friends or your family are beginning to say behind your back "it's about time "... for you to move on, heal, get over it, go out, ... basically they are meaning leave them alone, and stop talking about what your spouse did to shock and hurt you. They care about you and love you, but they want to start hearing you say something new or positive. They want you to start living your life again. This book is written to help you do just that. We have all been there, or should I say most of us in today's American society have. Even though fewer in the Christian community have, there are still more than everyone lets on. Just remember that you are not alone. This book is written to help you heal and move on with your life in a positive and constructive way.

Introduction

The design of this book is flexible and fluid enough that you, the reader, can go in and select a chapter or several chapters that you find appealing. It is not necessarily a book that you need to read from cover to cover, even though it is hoped that you will. You can open it up to a theme and focus on that area. You will find a format that is more appealing to you individually. There will be case studies, practical everyday psychology supported by theory, journal exercises, prayer journal exercises, and resources in each chapter.

You may like the everyday practical psychology, so that like me, you can remember the topic and use the application when the time occurs. Therefore, you may like to read the chapter in detail, pondering it as you reflect how this is related to your life. The chapter topic may cause you to begin to analyze why you do some of the things that you do. It may cause you to start to think of ways that you can make changes in your life. The new understanding of yourself and your actions may be something that you never took the time to analyze before.

Resources will be listed at the end of each chapter. I have found these to be most beneficial. You may want to go to those sources and read more. You may want to perform a more in depth study of the topic yourself. You may find in the bookstore or library that there is a book that appeals to you more than the ones listed. Take the time to look for many sources of help: books, web sites on the internet, movies, songs, etc. Make note of them on the NOTES pages provided. Or, you may just skip on to the next chapter because you do not need any more information on the topic. The resources are there to use if you desire more information on the topic.

Or, you may find case studies most appealing; the theory played out in real life situations. You may want to skim over the chapter and read the case study in depth. It is sometimes easier to read about someone else's life than to remember and live your own. Yet, as you read the case study you may not be able to avoid the similarities between you and the person being cited.

Others of you may like substance; you want to know the foundation found in theory. Just remember this is not a crash course in psychology. There is just enough theory cited in this book to give it some credibility and validity.

I find Ellis' Rational Emotive Therapy effective and believe that the best that comes out of theory is to put it into practice. Therefore, I like the journal exercises at the end of each of the chapters. These exercises are intended to take all of the theory and boil it down into a useful and simplistic form giving it meaning for you. In other words, helping you to figure out how this specifically plays out in your life. Most importantly, it makes you focus on issues that are important to you. I know from a standpoint of psychology that once a person thinks and commits by writing things down, and then focuses on them, the greater the chance is for making change and having the change last. Change is more likely to occur after these types of exercises than if you just think about the issues. The end of each chapter is there to help you question "How is this information going to benefit, heal, and/or enrich my life?" And that is the main reason you are reading this book. You are looking for a way to heal from the emotional pain of separation and divorce. Hopefully, you will take the time to use the journal exercises and not skim over them.

Because I am a faith-based individual and a Christian, I find my strength and meaning in Christ. Therefore, I have added the prayer journal exercises. You will find it helpful to get you focused on the ONE who truly loves YOU, GOD! Remember you are not alone. His spirit surrounds you with love and He binds the brokenhearted. The prayer journal can be used even if you are not a Christian. If you use meditation to find peace, I feel the exercises will still be beneficial to you.

So you pick and choose. My intent is to give you comfort and flexibility to meet your highly personal needs and interests. This book is not written for the therapist but is written for the lay person. The audience will for the most part be gender specific, mostly female, yet if you are a male going through the same situations as cited in this book, I am glad you can relate and hope that you benefit from the book, exercises, and resources.

Most women are wearing too many hats, doing too many jobs, carrying the world of work and family on their shoulders. If this is you, you are not taking time to meet some of your needs, especially when you are going through the horrors of divorce and separation. You may find you will have to hang up some of your hats while you are using this book. For instance, if you find yourself in the pediatrician's office waiting, or at the bus stop or anywhere there is a moments peace, you may pull out this little book and do a question or two of an exercise. No one will even realize you are working in a self-help book. They will probably think you are making a list to go shopping later. If enough time is what you don't seem to have, then take this book with you and use it wherever you find the time.

For others of you, time is all you have right now. Spend it wisely. Use it for reflection and improvement, not loneliness. Stop attending those pity parties; they can become addictive and are bad for your health. Seriously, use the resource list to branch out, gather information and search out divorced/separation recovery groups in your area to attend. Spend quality time using your journal and prayer journal exercises. You are fortunate to have this time to truly pull yourself back together, dust yourself off and live again.

During my divorce, I resided in a state were the process of divorce was lengthy. If the divorce was uncontested, the divorcing couple had to live apart for one year. After that time if divorce was still what they desired, they could follow through with the legal process. If the divorce was contested the length of time was two years before the difficult legal battle could proceed in the courts. In contrast, the state I reside in now only takes one month of separation for an uncontested divorce. I feel healing from the emotional pain of separation and divorce takes time. I have written the book with this healing time frame in mind. I feel the chapters and exercises should be completed slowly at a pace of one chapter per month. This, again, is a personal preference. You may find you can move faster than suggested due to the emotional distance that may have already transpired at the end of your marriage. Or, you may feel you need to work through this book on a slower pace than what I suggest. It is up to you to decide. You are your own best advocate when it comes to your personal healing time frame.

I hope you make good use of all the parts of this book in conjunction with each other and find yourself back on the road to wholeness. Good Luck!

Section One
Time

Chapter One
Healing

You will want to love again. Be sure to get your priorities straight before you begin. Begin with loving yourself first. When you have overflowing love for you, then love for others will spill over. This may in time spill over into dating and even finding the "right" person again. The goal is to love you. The rest will happen when you achieve your goal. I will write more about this in *Section Two - Love*. For right now, you will begin with taking the first step to healing. I will begin to direct you in this chapter, to analyze yourself, your need for healing, and your concepts regarding healing and the healthiness of others. All of these will affect your own healing and the time it will take.

The healthy don't need healing. Who is healthy? Are they really? Are they being honest with themselves? Healing is for those hurting. Many people are hurting in many ways. Healing can and will take time.

You have a unique opportunity. You have a broken heart. It is shattered into pieces. Some pieces are large and rather whole while others are small. It will take time to pick up all of these pieces. Time to lovingly and tenderly put them back together. As you pick up each piece, you will have this time in your life to take a close look at it. You can analyze it carefully and evaluate it. You can analyze its strength, wholeness, and need for repair. Some pieces will just need dusting off and polishing. Others need filler. Some may need a professional. You will be the judge

Before the separation and/or divorce took place you did not stop to look so closely at these pieces. You did not stop to analyze if there was a crack, flaw, or splinter. You just went about participating in a normal routine. This routine may not have been perfect, but it was life, your life. There may have been times that certain events or words were spoken which bumped into an area of your heart that was sore or tender. It happened so quickly that you did not even take notice. Other areas of your heart when touched seemed hard and cold. You would just direct or deflect the feelings. Who had time in your busy routine to stop and analyze every little sore spot?

Now, life has changed. Routine has stopped. Everything is being noticed. So take the time and use it wisely. As you pick up your pieces, see if there are cracks that can be filled in, splinters to be removed, and flaws to be professionally buffed out by a master. Given the right tools, you may be able to apply the fillers. Small cracks can disappear. Splinters may have caused festering. The area may need to be cleaned out, the splinter removed and antibiotic ointment applied. If the splinter has gone too deeply, a doctor will be required for treatment. A few trips to the doctor's office and all will be new. In the case of flaws, the doctor may refer you to a master professional that performs unique and lasting repair. Using this analogy, stop and analyze your pieces as you begin picking up each of them.

The hurting that is within you didn't happen quickly and wasn't just a one time incident. It happened repeatedly over time by many people, not just by your spouse telling you that he/she was leaving or physically moving out and away from your marriage and the home. I am asking you to begin your healing by taking a look back over your lifetime to see if any prior hurts and pains came from another time and relationship.

Some hurt, which happened over time, may have happened in your family relationships. It is rare in today's society for someone to grow up without experiencing some hurt, no matter how small. Your parents probably weren't perfect, and neither were your brothers and sisters. According to most psychologists, approximately 98% of families are dysfunctional in some way. This dysfunction usually means someone was hurt: physically, mentally, emotionally, or socially. If it didn't happen to you in your individual family setting growing up, maybe it did to your spouse. This type of pain and hurt can affect individual childhood development, as well as affect your marriage relationship.

You and/or your spouse may have been hurt in relationships outside the family settings growing up. Peer relationships may have contributed to some of your deep feelings about yourself. Childhood playmates are notorious for being cruel along with teen friends during those awkward years of maturity. Many adults still carry childhood pains around with them.

Your work mates may have contributed as well, by watering those seeds of doubt that were sown as a child. Feelings of self-doubt may have been fertilized by you or by your spouse, unintentionally. Maybe you or your spouse never communicated the pain that still existed or that was being caused at times in your relationship. Perhaps it was felt that if the subject were not addressed, it would go away on its own. In other words, heal. You may have harbored these feelings or possibly your spouse did without the other knowing what was really going on.

Other hurts may have developed over time in child/adult relationships outside the family. These child/adult relationships may have been with teachers, church leaders, troop leaders, etc. Some may have even been very seriously damaging in nature. Some of you reading this book may have been a victim of an abusive relationship in childhood and/or as an adult. I hope not, but this is a book of reality. You are no longer living in a fairy tale book of happily ever after if you are reading this. Please, don't put down this book. Persevere, persist and heal as you observe reality.

What I am trying to help you approach is getting rid of all your emotional pain and hurt, whenever and wherever it occurred. If you feel it would help your spouse, get an extra copy of this book so that you both can analyze your individual selves and maybe be able to come back together into a stronger marriage relationship. Treat your separation as just a bump in the road of life. For others, the reality will mean you need to pick up all your pieces, put them back together with loving care and move on to a new era in your life.

The purpose of this book is to get at those old and new hurts, deal with them once and for all, and HEAL. You may think you have never been hurt before this ending of your marriage, yet I still want you to look at your entire life: your childhood, your teen years, and your adult years and identify any thread of rejection and hurt. Observe the cracks, splinters, and flaws so that you can restore your heart to the beautiful wholeness THAT IS YOU!

The next chapter will cover more specifically these causes of "Hurts Over Time." Before moving on to the second chapter, I would like you to take the time to review the resources available to you. I have listed at the end of each chapter, ones that I found when I was going through my separation and divorce. I would like you to note others that you may have found. You might have a pamphlet or another book, which someone has given to you. Note it here at the end of the chapter to remind you to get back to it later. Also, be sure to make evaluative notes regarding its usefulness for later reference to help others.

If you haven't yet, you may want to go to my website, www. Healing After Divorce . com. At the website, there are several web pages of different material to supplement the book. There is a blog page to use to begin a virtual support group. Please make blog comments on the website as you read and work through the book. As others come online, you can all work together to dispel the feelings of aloneness. From time to time, I will add short articles that relate to the separated and divorced. Be sure to check back for those. When you have completed this workbook, remember to write your own evaluation using the comment form.

Now, read the first case study and see if any of the life events correlate with yours. And then think about writing your own one page case study. What would you write about you?

Next, it will be time to move on to the first journal and journaling exercises. These beginning exercises are simple and an easy way to get started on your healing journey. Good Luck, God Bless, and God Speed.

NOTES

Chapter One – Healing
RESOURCES

Movies (dvd, tv, etc.)

Songs

Books/Articles/Other Resources
(and articles on the internet)

Nehemiah Notes- April 15, 2004 "Confronting The Fear Of Change", Nehemiah Ministries, Inc., Blaine Smith, Director, P.O. Box 448, Damascus, MD 20872 www . nehemahministries. com

Organizations

Fresh Start Seminars, P.O. Box 968, Duluth, GA 30096

Psychiatrists, Psychotherapists, and Psychologists
Robert Ellis and Rational Emotive Therapy

List any resources you have found and used so far.

Movies_____
_____

Songs_____
_____

Articles_____
_____
_____

Organizations_____
_____

Psychiatrists, Psychotherapists, and Psychologists recommended by friends or in your phone book

_____

How did these resources relate to you and your situation?

_____
_____
_____
_____
_____
_____
_____
_____
_____
_____

Case Study #1

Jane was a 32 year-old, middle class, school teacher going through a divorce. She had stopped attending church because she felt no one there could relate to her situation. All the people she knew were married couples. She had no single friends. Some of her previous friends had sided with her husband and some remained with her camp. Yet, no one invited her over for dinner more than the first time shortly after the separation took place.

She no longer cried herself to sleep as she did in the beginning. Food just didn't taste good anymore. She had dropped a lot of weight. She had always been someone who needed at least eight hours of sleep each night to function, but for months now she couldn't sleep for more than 6 hours, and those were hours of interrupted light sleep. No one wanted to hear about her situation anymore. If she began to talk about it, her friends would all of a sudden have to go or would change the topic and not let her come to a conclusion. She was feeling cut off and very alone. TV programs couldn't hold her interest. Movies and novels could not transport her to another place and time. She just could not escape from her life and her emotional pain.

A fellow teacher in her school had finally heard, by a slow route of gossip, that she was separated from her husband. He gave her a brochure to a seminar coming to his church. It was a ministry for separated and divorced people. It was designed to help hurting people. The seminar ran from a Friday night until Saturday evening. There was a registration fee, which she felt was expensive, but Jane decided to do it. Later she realized that this became a turning point in her life. She found people living in her town, whom she had never seen before, who were hurting just like her. Some of the men and women traveled hours to come to this seminar, which was held once a year at this church. The sessions consisted of large-group general talks, and then small-group talk sessions. Jane found others felt just like her, they were going through similar situations and adjustments as she was.

After the seminar, she discovered the church had Friday night sessions each week for persons going through separation. They had one rule to belong, and that was that you were separated, once you were divorced you had to move on to a different group they had for singles. They did not want their ministry to be a singles dating scene. She began attending the Friday night sessions and soon her feelings of aloneness went away. She began to sleep better and food became appetizing again. The healing process had begun.

People want to love, to be loved, and to have a sense of belonging. Jane may not be in love and her husband no longer loved her, but she found persons with whom she could identify. She had a sense of belonging.

Chapter One - Healing
Journal

This is your first journaling section of the book. Use it in conjunction with meditation, prayer, devotion and reflection. Be sure to be honest with yourself. You do not need to show this to anyone. Please write down your answers because you will be coming back to them later to reflect and work on healing in later chapters. If there is nothing written, it will be hard for you to remember what you had reflected on the day you worked on this chapter.

When I was personally going through divorce, I rarely wrote my thoughts down, but when I did I found that pages would come pouring out of me when I didn't think there was anything that I wanted to write. For some of you like me, you may need to keep a spiral notebook to use along with this book. Be sure to title your pages so you can refer to them later. Make your comments on Notes pages.

Okay let's get started. Roll up those emotional sleeves because they may get a little dirty as we begin this hard work. Get your pen or pencil and put on your thinking cap.

Who exactly am I?

Right now? Or who do I want to be? Right now I'm just a little girl who wants to be picked, loved, cherished, and poured into with love and protection. I never saw myself as beautiful or worthy or even honorable. Something about the stigma of not being able to carry a child has always made me feel less than a woman. Who am I? Someone learning to love herself - every part. Every broken part of herself.

Why am I going through this emotional pain?
because I am hurting and it's a part of the process to greive what is no longer there. I am also alone, but I am NOT really alone. I have God and the people who care about me. But I also have to care about myself.

How did this happen?
We both had a role in this and I gave up on believing he could ever be truthful and I gave up on believing in him and respecting him and probably loving him.

What am I looking for in reading and using this book?
Healing

Where can I turn for help?
GOD.

When do I plan on setting aside time to read and work in my book?

Daily

Write a first draft of a case study about you. Describe yourself in an opening paragraph.

Chavez is an adventurer at heart and a life long seeker of knowledge/truth. She enjoys reading and traveling and being surrounded by family and friends. She doesn't have too many close friends. She loves hard but doesn't have a lot of people who love her like that.

Describe your childhood through young adult years mentioning experiences that had a profound influence on you as a person.

Describe your experiences regarding separation.

_____
_____
_____
_____
_____
_____
_____
_____
_____
_____

Describe your experiences regarding the divorce if you have already gone through this stage.

_____
_____
_____
_____
_____
_____
_____
_____
_____
_____

Remember this is only a first draft not a final case study on you. By the time you are finished with this book you will probably write it differently anyway.

Chapter One – Healing
Prayer Journal

If you are a faith based or spiritually motivated person, I suggest you keep a separate journal. The second journal will be a prayer/devotion journal. Keep it beside your bed. Work on it first thing in the morning or last thing at night. I found this to be most helpful during my separation year. I set the alarm clock an hour earlier to spend some very serious time with the one that I knew truly loved me ... My God!

Here is my suggestion of how to get started: Buy a small spiral notebook. Date each page as you use it at the top for referencing some day down the road. You may come back to the page to see how God has worked in your life through prayer and devotion. You may find prayers answered that you had forgotten about. You may be amazed how quickly they were answered or how the answer was actually NO. You may find that the answers came many years later and marvel how God's plan was working all the time to reach your hoped for outcome. It is important to date the page.

First, list things for which you are thankful.

Thank God for them.

Next, list prayer needs for you specifically.

Pray for yourself.

Then list prayer needs for others.

Pray for those you have listed by name and need.

Pray for guidance in selecting a scripture passage or devotional reading.

Lastly, express thanks to God again.

Turn to a scripture passage or in a devotion book and read and reflect.

List the passage.

Then reflect on how it fed you spiritually (what commonality you found with the written words).

On the next page you will find a sample page for you to use to get started setting up your special prayer/devotion book. I am confident that over the years you will reflect upon this time as the most precious moments that you can remember. The time spent will be well worth it. When I look back on those years for me, I find that I consider them bittersweet. The separation/divorce was painful but my special time with my Lord and Savior was so sweet. Which reminds me of an old hymn that was sung in my church as a child: "'Tis so sweet to trust in Jesus." I pray that you find this true for you.

Date: _____

Prayer: Things for which I am thankful _____

Prayer: For my specific needs _____

Prayer: For

    Others   Needs

    _____   _____

    _____   _____

    _____   _____

    _____   _____

Scripture led to: _____

How was I fed (How did I relate to the passage)?

_____

_____

NOTES

Section One
Time

Chapter Two
Hurt Over Time

As I stated before, your personal pains or hurts in life have happened repeatedly over time and were your reaction to life events involving a variety of people. Remember, according to psychology textbooks approximately 98% of families are dysfunctional in some way. This dysfunction usually means someone was hurt: physically, mentally, emotionally, or socially. And it may mean that is you. I will begin with the emotional hurts.

Emotional hurts may have been formed in your family relationships when you were a child. They may have been formed due to an "overbearing" parental relationship or by just the opposite, the lack of parental/child relationship. Hurts may have happened as the result of a child's distorted concept of reality. I must make one thing clear before I go on with this topic. The purpose of this book is not to bash or blame anyone. This book was written to help you analyze some of your past and present life events, evaluate any pain and damage stemming from that time period, and assess if that hurt is so damaging that it needs to be addressed so it can be healed properly. Maybe it needs a new type of medication or medical procedure in order for it to heal correctly. Think of this as plastic surgery. You may have healed from past emotional injuries, but it may have left a very ugly scar or has disfigured you beyond recognition. It is time to lovingly remove the scar and help the area to heal so that it no longer is visible, therefore, affecting how you relate to others and yourself at this time.

As you matured you built your self-esteem. Emotional hurts may cause you to build low or poor self-esteem. Self-esteem is similar to a brick structure. The blocks, whether made with small bricks or large cinder blocks, are all held together with mortar. This composition is important. The self-esteem is rated by the mortar that holds it all together. If the mortar is a good mix of the correct elements, it will last many years and can withstand all types of weather (relationships) and storms (experiences) that come along. On the other hand, if the mortar is a poor mix, the wall may suffer fatigue and sometimes portions of the wall will collapse and brick will need rebuilding.

Keeping with this analogy, most of the mortar was made in your childhood years and the blocks were laid over time. Your relationship with your parents or the caregivers that raised you formed the mortar. Positive words, proper discipline and balanced love built a strong foundation for your structure of self-esteem. If parenting skills were poor or lacking, the foundation may have been weak and unable to support the rest of the building. Even when all that has been built after the early years of life has been perfectly laid, a strong foundation is still necessary.

The foundation to your structure of self-esteem is very important. Negative, unloving, uncaring, neglectful parents have a profound effect on the child's future and on the child's ability to form good working habits and relationships, as well as interpersonal relationships with friends, spouses and children. In all fairness, some parents have and are doing the best they can; if they could have done better they would have done so. Remember parents built your parents' foundations. They learned parenting skills from their parents. Your parents either mimicked their parents in raising you or they have been doing their best to parent you differently from the way they were parented. There is no parenting manual out there that comes with each individual child. Each child is unique and needs a unique raising guide. The child's disposition, personality, demeanor, birth placement, etc. all affect how that particular child should be properly parented. To learn more about child psychology you will need to read works by Jean Piaget, a French child psychologist.

Now, examine your foundations. We all have memories of a good and/or bad time with our mother, our father or with both. Some memories are all too vividly remembered. These memories are stored amazingly in video or audio tape format in your brain, and you may play them back on occasion. These "tapes" reveal the type of mortar mix that I have been talking about. You may still be playing those negative tapes in your head even though you are 40, 50, or 60 years of age. These negative tapes help to undermine the way you feel about yourself and react and relate to others around you. These negative tapes reveal what made up the poor mix of mortar. You may hear yourself say or play these tapes when you perform certain tasks. You may hear them as what is called "self talk." You have played those original negative tapes so many times they are worn out and should have been discarded. You don't need the original voices on tape anymore, you believe it so much that you naturally say it in your own voice to yourself. These comments originally formed your foundation. These comments either made the foundation weak or made it a strong self-esteem foundation.

If you find your self-talk is always negative and that your foundation of self-esteem is weak there is Good News! It is not too late. You can begin re-taping the negative tapes into new parenting tapes for yourself, making a much stronger mortar for your self-esteem foundation. Some foundations were done perfectly and as I have pointed out others were not. I will write more about this in later chapters. For now, I want you to become aware that it exists and begin to consciously notice it.

Now look at some of your self-esteem structure. When your parents weren't looking your siblings and close playmates were laying some block. Those siblings and playmates may also be responsible for some of the bad mortar and negative tapes. Since sibling rivalry exists, (even sometimes all through your life) I cannot over emphasize this part of your structure building. Your birth order and your placement in the family, your gender, and your own personality may have affected the way you formed your self-esteem structure and possibly its foundation. There is much written by many psychologists regarding the forming of our personalities. Think of it this way, you are the cement mixer and many ingredients were deposited into the mixer and you churned out your mortar. The great thing is that you own the mixer as well as the structure and you can go back and tweak the mortar mix and make appropriate adjustments anytime you want. Other parts of the mortar are permanent and are really okay the way they are. Either way, what I would like you to do is to take a close look at your mortar and structure.

Some questions I am asking you to think about are… Were you the oldest? Were you given too much responsibility at too young an age? Did your parents have gender prejudices that restrained you from activities and pushed you into others that would have been beneficial or harmful to your development as you now view it? Or were you the youngest and always picked on by your older sibling? Did you learn that no one trusted you to be responsible causing you not to be? Were you always being compared to your older sibling and never seemed to measure up? Or were you the middle child with no clear-cut role to play? Were you sometimes in charge and then other times not?

Were you an easygoing, trusting, compliant child who had overbearing, overprotective parents? Or were you the child that needed to test the limits? Were you the child that just needed to know how far you would be allowed to go before your parents would show you enough love to finally discipline you? Now back to your structure.

This part of your self-esteem structure is permanently built. The mortar has hardened. It could be blasted out and rebuilt, yet for the most part it is a strong structure and can be used the way it is. Actually, it has caused you to have very good mortar and an excellent structure of self-esteem. It would not be worth bringing in a demolition crew and starting over. Freudian psychology tends to have this effect. Other psychology methods feel there are better results in less time without starting completely over. Instead, you just need to examine the structure and check the mortar. If you become aware of defects that are severe, you can patch the areas with professional help and maintain the structure as viable. You can repair less severe cracks using self-help approaches. In this chapter's journal exercise, you will answer some of the above questions, as well as others. In later chapter journals, I will suggest ways for you to patch some of your weak mortar.

At this time, take a look at some more of the structure. The next builders were your childhood peers, your playmates and close friends. Heaven knows they were not qualified to do the work, but none the less they did. Some more questions to ask yourself are: Were you a loner? Did you have one very influential friend? Were you gregarious and had numerous friends? Or were you part of a neighborhood group of children? Were your inner needs for affirmation met? Did others your own age criticize you? Were you often openly rejected? Did you learn to cope?

Your work peers assist in this portion of your structure by affirming and denying your *self* worth. By now, at your current age, these work peers don't have influence on the permanent mortar. They may apply a mortar patch now and again or chip a little of the mortar away, but they don't affect your structure as much as your childhood peers did.

The frequency of affirmation or denial of your *self* worth in your childhood years determined this mortar mix. This phase of your self-esteem construction could be very fragile. It may need some under-girding to strengthen it, especially when experiencing separation and/or divorce. After all, your spouse was your Ultimate Peer. The journals and resources lists are designed to help you. I invite you again to take the time to use them.

Your next masons/brick layers may have laid bricks unevenly. These masons may have been poorly trained and had not passed the test for laying blocks correctly. They may have been educated and trained, but lacked the natural skill to do the job properly. These masons were other adults, such as teachers, church leaders, troop leaders, club sponsors and the like. The adult/child relationships were your first confirmation or denial that what your parents were telling you each day through actions and words about yourself were true or not. Sometimes this means your mortar mix was different in consistency, color, and strength. The more the mortar matched that prepared by your parents the stronger your good or the weaker your bad self-esteem structure was built.

You may have even experienced abuse causing you to question your self-worth. The abuse may have happened as a child and continued through adult years or it may have appeared only during your adult years in a relationship of marriage. There are several types of abuse: physical abuse, sexual abuse, and emotional/mental (usually in the form of verbal) abuse. If it ever happened, one thing is sure, it never will be forgotten and you know you do not want it to happen again!

If it has never happened to you, you may think it can never happen to you. You may think that it only happens to weak and stupid people. Don't be deceived. Strangers can cause abuse but it mostly happens in relationships. When it does happen to you, you are embarrassed and don't want anyone to know. That is how abuse continues. Abuse feeds and grows through isolation and secrecy. If or when it begins you must tell the world and run like Hell. If you don't, it will repeat over and over again. Abuse only ends when one person dies or the relationship ends.

Physical abuse may be the result of alcohol abuse. Under the influence of alcohol, the spouse becomes enraged and physically abusive. Sometimes the relationship can be saved and physical abuse ends because the spouse gives up alcohol. The spouse realizes they are an addict and seeks help through Alcoholics Anonymous. The family gets counseling through Al-Anon. You may have been a child that grew up in this type of household. If so, another good source of healing can come from Adult Children of Alcoholics. It would be wonderful to blame all physical abuse on alcohol addiction only because if you take away the alcohol, you take away the abuse. This is like a fairy godmother approach with a magic wand and everyone lives happily ever after, but this is not always true. Some spouses go into a fit of rage and become physically abusive without the aid of alcohol. The abused over time becomes paranoid trying to guess by trial and error what to do or not do to avoid the inevitable flying object, verbal insults, and physical pain from pushing, slapping, hitting, punching, or twisting of limbs. The abuser always convinces the abused the next day that they are so sorry, they really love them, and to please not leave them. And so it goes on.

Always linked with physical abuse is emotional/mental abuse, but physical abuse is not always present with emotional/mental abuse. This is the ultimate use of negative tape playing. Terms of endearment or should I say terms of UN-endearment are degrading names. There are many examples. Some are: "slut", "whore", "tramp", "bit__ or bast___", etc. and worse. More mentally degrading phrases regarding accomplishments or performance are: "you will never amount to anything," "you can't do anything right," "who taught you how to ... ," "you are as worthless as... ," " "how stupid can you get," "if you can't do it right don't do it at all," etc. After many years of hearing this type of talk you feel unlovable, unworthy of love, and not good enough to deserve better. You are left not having the strength to even leave such a damaging relationship because it has undermined your mortar so badly and the bricks are laying all around whatever wall is still standing.

Sexual abuse is an attack much more damaging than the physical abuse, even though it often is physically damaging. It is such a personal attack. Those of you who were abused may have recessed into a deep world within yourself. You no longer feel that you live in a safe and protected world. It may take many years for you to see yourself as a sexual being without fear of being attacked again. So you paint your wall the ugliest battleship gray and hope no one ever casts an eye your way.

Abuse can leave permanent damage and scarring to the self-esteem. This is definitely an area on which "plastic surgery" by a therapist is needed to remove the emotional scarring. I truly pray you do not need a real plastic surgeon for outward physical scarring, too. But the scarring of self worth brought on by sexual abuse needs a good therapist specializing in sexual abuse to help you repair the inward scarring. I can not emphasize this enough. Do not be afraid of getting good professional help.

If abuse has happened to you, *Please, Please, Please **seek professional help***. Love yourself even if no one else has ever truly loved you by demonstrating a caring love. Maybe you have experienced all of the forms of abuse I have mentioned here, know that you are not alone. It happens to more people than you can imagine. I have experienced more than one form of the abuse I have written about in this chapter. Through education and/or personal experience I know what damage can occur if you do not seek help. If you are one of the victims of abuse that I have so briefly described, I want you to heal those old wounds so that you can go on with life. I know we all (abused and unabused) deserve to live a happy and productive life.

In conclusion, relationships over a lifetime consist of Parent/Child, Child/Child, Adult/Child, and Adult/Adult relationships. Relationships by nature usually result in emotional closeness. Emotional closeness or the lack of it, in the relationship context, helps us to form our self-esteem, be it good or bad. Painful experiences may have caused you to form a poor self-esteem i.e. to feel poorly about yourself. If you are encouraged in relationships to feel good about yourself and your abilities, then you develop good self-esteem. Remember that poor self-esteem does not need to be a permanent condition. It is repairable. You owe it to yourself to develop a good self-esteem, whether built in childhood or now in adulthood.

NOTES

Chapter Two - Hurt Over Time
RESOURCES

Movies (dvd, tv, etc.)

Sleeping with the Enemy (1991)
(This is not recommended for the abused, this is recommended only for the unabused so you can understand and support the abused better)

Songs

Earl by Dixie Chicks

This Love Is A Love That Never Walks Away by Kathy Troccoli
www.kathytroccoli.com.

Books/Articles/Groups/Other Resources
(and articles on the internet)

Dobson, Ph.D., James. Radio host of *Focus on the Family* has written many books that can be research at the website
http://www.focusonthefamily.com/

Organizations

Alcoholics Anonymous
Al-Anon
Adult Children of Alcoholics

Psychiatrists, Psychotherapists, and Psychologists

For quick study of Theories of Psychology
http://www.psy.pdx.edu/PsiCafe/KeyTheorists

List any resources you have found and used so far.

How did this resource relate to you and your situation?

Case Study #2

Charlene was the only child of her parents. During her elementary school years, she grew up in a large city. Her parents then bought property and built a very nice home in a small rural town, where she finished her school years. She excelled in high school and was an excellent reader. She attended a college for 1 ½ yrs. making fine grades. She then dropped out and returned home. She dated a boy from her hometown. He had his own business and they settled down. She had one son and was elected to be the town mayor. Time went by and they separated and divorced.

During her single mom years she had been employed by a company and had an excellent position, but it required long hours on the computer. She developed carpal tunnel syndrome, was operated on, and was forced to retire with disability and in much pain. She developed fibromyalgia and began receiving social security disability. About 10 years had gone by, and her ex-husband began to woo her back into a relationship. They got back together. She would not get remarried though. He had been physically abusive before and she was afraid to get totally reconnected to him again, yet she still loved him. As feared, the abuse began again after he had spun his web of deceit and false hope. He had her right where he wanted her---pregnant, under his control, cut off again from any outside support, having one 10 year old who wanted his dad around, and no means of self-worth affirming activities.

Ten more years passed. He'd be gone for days and had excuses to cover his absence. She discovered on Thanksgiving Day that her ex-mother-in-law had helped him keep a secret. The mother-in-law had invited Charlene and her two sons to late Thanksgiving dinner and the new wife and baby to early dinner. Their paths crossed in the driveway. That gave Charlene enough anger to leave him and cut ties with the ex-mother-in-law and try to get back on her own again. That meant she had to buy him out of half of the house they had purchased. Her oldest son was now old enough to work and assist her with the buy out. The son realized how harmful this was to his mother and would try to protect her. They were able to buy him out, but not before he came to the house and threatened her at gun point. He ended up knocking her into a door jamb so hard he gave her a concussion and had her in the hospital for days. She was able to get a restraining order and lived in severe fear for months until the buy out. A few years have passed at this point, and it seems he is not interested in his first family now as much as the new one.

Remember if you have gotten away with your life the first time, don't be fooled again. Learn and be able to quote Gal 5:1.

Stand fast therefore in the liberty wherewith Christ hath made us free, and be not entangled again with the yoke of bondage.
Gal 5:1 (KJV)

Chapter Two – Hurt Over Time
Journal

In the chapter one journal exercise I told you to roll up those emotional sleeves because they may get a little dirty as you begin this hard work. You may need to now put on rubber gloves to handle some of the stuff you may dig up. It may have been buried for quite awhile and hasn't seen the light of day for some time. It may have festered and rotted, and be rather smelly. The main thing to be mindful of as you handle these items is not to re-live them. Act like a mirror that reflects and doesn't feel, as if these things happened to someone else.

1. What is your earliest memory? Think hard back to before you went to school if possible. How old were you? Who else is in the memory? Where did it take place? Describe the memory with as many details as possible.

_____
_____
_____
_____
_____
_____
_____
_____
_____

2. Describe any memory that you have regarding your parents that you feel influenced your self-esteem building.

_____
_____
_____
_____
_____
_____
_____
_____

3. Describe any memory that you have regarding your siblings that you feel influenced your self-esteem building.

_____
_____
_____
_____
_____
_____
_____
_____

4. Describe any memory that you have regarding your childhood friends that you feel influenced your self-esteem building.

_____
_____
_____
_____
_____
_____
_____
_____

5. Describe any memory that you have regarding other adults in your childhood that you feel influenced your self-esteem building.

_____
_____
_____
_____
_____
_____
_____
_____

6. Describe any memory that you have regarding your teen friends that you feel influenced your self-esteem building.

_____
_____
_____
_____
_____
_____
_____
_____
_____

7. What memory of the past regarding your self-esteem has been confirmed in your adulthood?

_____
_____
_____
_____
_____
_____
_____
_____
_____

8. List your traits, abilities, accomplishments, interests, talents and gifts.

_____
_____
_____
_____
_____
_____
_____
_____
_____

NOTES

Chapter Two – Hurt Over Time
Prayer Journal

You have already been keeping your prayer journal in a separate little notebook. Of course, I do not want you to stop. I want you to remember specific others in your prayers now that you have completed your Chapter Two Journal exercise.

Thank the Lord for your unique personality and traits.

Thank the Lord specifically for each of the persons that you wrote about when remembering your childhood.

Thank the Lord for how each of the persons that you wrote about shaped your life (whether for better or the worse).

Ask the Lord to give you a clear mind to recall anything more that you should remember that would assist you at this time in your life.

Ask the Lord to help you through any painful memories that may have been unburied and for understanding of the purpose.

Thank the Lord for always being with you.

Thank the Lord for not being alone because the Lord is always with you and to be mindful that all you need to do is call upon Him.

Read the following scripture passages related to Chapter Two "Hurt Over Time". Note your thoughts on each theme area after reading all the passages of scripture given.

Theme

Stop the Continuing Cycle of Abuse
Psm. 18:16-19; Psm. 12:18; Psm. 10:12; Prov. 11:29; Matt.18:6

_____
_____
_____
_____

Give Loving Support
Heb. 13:1; 1 Cor. 12:26

_____
_____
_____
_____

Know You Are Not Alone
Matt. 1:23; Gen. 45

_____
_____
_____
_____

Gain Strength
Phil. 4:13

_____
_____
_____
_____

Section One
Time

Chapter Three
Healing Takes Time

In the last chapter I had you think about the hurts that have taken place or formed over a lifetime. Now I will begin to address ways to repair, fix, and therefore heal those areas. This process will take time. It can't be done over night, but you only need to take one step at a time.

In order to make repairs to the self-esteem structure, you need to mix the new mortar. The components or ingredients to your mortar recipe are very important, along with the mixing techniques. Components of a good mix are:

Love

   Patience

      Positive Awareness

         Centeredness

            Belief

               Tenderness

                  Self-Talk

There is no proper order to gathering these ingredients. They just need to exist. Like using any recipe, it becomes better as you develop just the right mix for you. It is a personal recipe for self-esteem mortar. The recipe may have been used to form your original structure, but life's events may be responsible for chipping away some of the mortar. Or, your "old family" recipe may have been lost and now you want to find a recipe that is similar to the original one. For some, the original mix may have been faulty and a new mix is needed to add strength, so you will go around searching and trying out different recipes until you find a good one. Then, you will begin customizing it to suit your personal needs.

I will now discuss the importance of each of these ingredients and the mixing techniques. Later, I will have you consider the amounts needed.

One ingredient that you already know goes into the mix is LOVE. There is your love of your *self* and there is love that is shown to you by others. Remember, not enough is as dangerous as too much. Of course, proper proportions are as important as having the ingredient. As the saying goes, "too much of a good thing can be bad." It is also said, "you can't get enough love." Love that is known as "spoiling" is the type I am meaning when I say there can be too much. There is much to be said about Love. Therefore, I have devoted the next section of the book to the topic of Love.

"PATIENCE is a virtue." "Don't pray for patience because if you do, God will give you something to be patient about." These are two sentences often heard in church settings. Whether you are patient or impatient, you must be patient when you have no choice, like it or not. You can stomp your feet, cry at a feverish pitch, and display a temper tantrum, but it won't make time go by any faster or go backward to a happier time. Instead you need to develop a positive way to pass time, a way to be patient regarding your journey called life. Remember, it's the journey that counts, not the destination. If you pass time patiently by concentrating on healing, you will find that you will look back on a precious special time, even if you always remember it as a time of emotional pain. Like good dark chocolate, it will be bittersweet. Realize you are in a special precious time of your life. A time that is special and precious because you are having an intimate encounter with your "self." The next three chapters will go into detail about the **bittersweet chocolate era** of your life.

POSITIVE AWARENESS is another ingredient in the self-esteem mortar mix. Many people go through life without ever being aware of anything. It is as if they have blinders on or are programmed to perform. They bury feelings as well as awareness. You have heard it said, " wake up and smell the roses." The " wake up" is the "becoming aware." People walk past "roses" everyday and never register that they should "stop and smell." You are probably all too aware that you are in pain right now, but what else are you aware of? This is also stated in scripture:

Be still, and know that I am God. Psalm 46:10a (KJV)

When you are still, you can become aware. This silence and new awareness can give you a feeling of wholeness.

Awareness is noticing...noticing things that you sense: smell, touch, see, hear and taste. Positive awareness is finding the awe-someness feature about something. After you become practiced in using positive awareness, you become positively aware of feelings/emotions. Usually, when you discover these awe filled things and emotions you become thankful. This positive awareness is needed to repair the cracks or weak areas of your self-esteem structure.

Positive awareness brings about a CENTEREDNESS that is necessary for the mortar mixing. It is a drying agent. It makes the mortar harden and set up. Besides helping with the drying time, the ingredient of positive awareness also holds other added benefits. Children often have this ingredient; very small and insignificant things awe them. Over time as you age, with more responsibilities and demands, you forget that you ever possessed this ingredient in your original mortar mix. Without this ingredient, your mortar could dry over a longer time through air-drying or sun-drying. Yet the added benefits would be missing. Evidence of this centeredness is more positive self-awareness. It may cause you to laugh at and with your *self*. It is a peace that you feel within. Some still have that intact even though the separation knocked you down, while others of you are still searching for this peace. Some find it through having a divine love fill them. Centeredness and peace go hand in hand. Practice becoming aware. Re-center your *self*. Appreciate something very small and insignificant and smile at its beauty, its complexity, or its simplicity. Don't bypass the simple joy that you can experience and have so easily and freely. Wake up and see what you can be re-aware of or newly aware of. And don't forget to smile or even chuckle if a small emotional impulse asks you to stretch your face into a big grin.

     BELIEF, faith, trust, and knowing are all words connected to the fifth ingredient needed for the mortar mix. It can be belief and faith in God who sees and knows all, or Jesus who understands rejection. It can be belief in yourself because you know that you are worthy because your Creator made you and loves you. It can be a trust that all will be okay again someday soon. Or, you may call this a knowing inside, an intuition, or the Holy Spirit, that tells you that you are a valuable human and worthy of love. It can be a scripture verse that you claim as your own. For example:

I can do all things through Christ that strengtheneth me
Phil.4:13 (KJV)

Great is thy faithfulness Lam. 3:23 (KJV)

Yea, though I walk through the valley of the shadow of death I will fear no evil, for thou art with me
Psalm 23:4a (KJV)

Whatever it is, you know it gives you an inner strength, confidence, assurance and affirmation.

     TENDERNESS is an ingredient that comes about as you give yourself time to gather the other ingredients. Tenderness is the way to stir the ingredients together. It is a folding technique. In recipes that called for beaten egg whites or whipping cream, folding is necessary to keep from losing the precious air that is needed to make the final product light and fluffy. Tenderness stirs the mix, but it does it very gently so that you don't damage your preciously gathered ingredients. Tenderness will also be discussed later in detail in Section Three. It is as important as love and also deserves a section devoted to the topic.

SELF-TALK is important to the mixture I am calling mortar. It is not really an ingredient either, but a technique in the mixing of the recipe. It is like kneading a dough mixture for bread. The kneading develops elastic like strands called glutton to hold the bread together while baking. Self-talk is needed for your self-esteem mortar mix. Self-Talk was mentioned in the last chapter. It is your "old tapes" that you play over and over again. Previously, I referred to rewriting or re-taping those and now I will go into depth.

Self-talk helps you to lift yourself up or let yourself down. Some of those statements that need to be rewritten or re-taped are the ones that keep you from becoming all you were meant to be. God gifted all of you. If you don't feel that way, then your self-talk is getting in the way.

To re-tape you need to first play and write down those negative words. You need to then look at them and rewrite the words into a positive affirming statement. Then, say that statement out loud to your *self* and ask, "is it true." Do you want others to know or observe that this is true about you?
Examples

Old tape:	Rewrite:
I'm stupid	I'm smart
I can't	I'm capable
I'm ugly	I'm attractive

If, when you hear the new statement you say, "well, yeah, but..." then you need to find a middle ground statement that you can say to your *self* "yes, that is true, that's really me." As time goes on you may have to update these new tapes, because you now believe that you are more than the rewritten statement is saying to you. This may happen as you regain some of your self-esteem. When that time comes, don't hesitate. Rewrite and re-tape a new positive statement. And start playing those tapes.

The journal exercises of this chapter are going to work on rewrites of affirming self-talk for the re-taping.

Chapter Three - Healing Takes Time
RESOURCES

Movies (dvd, tv, etc.)

Osteen, Joel (May 28, 2006). *Giving Your Dreams a New Beginning*, Broadcast #307 Joel Osteen Ministries, www.joelosteen.com .

Songs

Books/Articles/Groups/Other Resources
(and articles on the internet)

De Mello, Anthony (1990). *Awareness,* New York: Doubleday. ISBN: 0-385-24937-3

De Mello, Anthony (1984). *Wellsprings, a Book of Spiritual Exercises,* New York: Doubleday. ISBN: 0-385-19617-2

Smith, Blaine (April 15, 2004). *Confronting the Fear of Change*, Nehemiah Ministries.

Psychiatrists, Psychotherapists, and Psychologists

Alfred Adler
Robert Ellis

NOTES

Case Study #3

Karen was born into a blue-collar family. She was the oldest and had one brother. Her parents were very strict and demanded complete conformity to their rules through physical punishment. She was a compliant child and conformed very willingly. At age 7, she had surgery and much eye therapy to correct a crossed eye. The eye surgeon considered it a miracle of a success. Her parents moved to a suburban area from the city within months of the surgery. This meant a new school, new classmates and neighbor children, and a patch and glasses. She was in the slowest reading group in her new second grade class. Throughout her school years, she had difficulty with her reading speed and comprehension. She had great difficulty with reading quietly in class if there was any noise or disruption in the classroom. Today, Karen thinks it may have been attention deficit. She developed a sense of stupidity, and fear of failure as a result of her reading problems.

Karen's mother encouraged her to work hard at her studies at home which was a quiet environment. She was interested in math and her childhood goal was to be a math teacher. In high school, she took academic courses and foreign language in order to meet college requirements. Karen was in the top 10% of her graduating class. She took trigonometry and pre-calculus and failed to make the A's that she had previously been accustomed to earning. She did not like to fail, and would rather not try than to fail. So, she selected something other than the math that she was interested in for a college major and teaching career. Years later, she pursued the math courses again in hopes of teaching math. She took college Calculus I and II and received A's. She found the subject boring to teach and was glad she had pursued her other interest for a teaching career.

She later earned a master's degree. In her graduate level psychology courses, she began to analyze her self-concept. Through remembering, reflecting, and rewriting some of those childhood memories, and in some cases discarding childhood distortions of reality, she was able to begin to believe she was intelligent and capable. She looked at her accomplishments and her goals and began to truly strive to achieve her "full" potential. Karen began to believe in and to love herself. She finally accepted the fact that she was not stupid.

Even though you may look at others and think they feel good about themselves because of what you see, they may not really have a good self-esteem, as was true of Karen. Karen had built a wall of weak self-esteem and later learned to repair the mortar and regain a strong and healthy wall of self-esteem. She rewrote and re-taped her self-talk tapes and began believing in her abilities and reached her potential.

NOTES

Chapter Three - Healing Takes Time
Journal

In this chapter journal exercise you are going to work on those "old tapes". Remember the mirroring technique when playing these tapes. During this exercise just reflect and don't feel. Act as if these things are being said to someone else.

1. What is the tape you most often hear in your head when things go wrong? Write down the words exactly as you hear them. Then list several different times or situations when you might hear this tape played.

_____
_____
_____
_____
_____
_____
_____
_____
_____
_____
_____
_____
_____
_____
_____
_____
_____
_____

2. Write new words for a new tape that can affirm you positively. Test the sound of these words for their accuracy when related to you. Test them out in the situations you have stated above. Does the new tape fit the situations? If not, write another tape, remembering to say it aloud for accuracy and testing it until you find the right words for the tape. Once you have the right words, write them here ten times. Now say all the lines until you have said all ten. Hint: Usually the sentence is short.

First draft

_____
_____

Second draft

_____
_____

Final draft

_____
_____

2 _____
_____

3 _____
_____

4 _____
_____

5 _____
_____

6 _____
_____

7 _____
_____

8 _____
_____

9 _____
_____

10 _____
_____

3. Describe how you felt after hearing the tapes ten times. Describe how these tapes would influence your self-esteem building.

4. Repeat the first journal exercise with another tape and other situations. Rewrite those words, remembering to test them for effect. Record them ten times.

5. Write the words of your new tapes. Post this list by your bathroom mirror, full-length mirror and any other place that your reflection can be seen. Then each time you look in that mirror, play your new tapes aloud for yourself to hear. If you have a tape recorder, actually record these tapes with the statements repeated ten times each. Play the tape to yourself each morning with coffee, in your car, and each evening before bed.

Warning! Do not sell yourself short. Complete these journal exercises even though you may feel they are odd, silly, or ridiculous. They are very powerful. It took many years to play and etch on your memory the first self-tapes regarding your self-esteem that you currently are using as your self-talk. **Healing Takes Time** and you deserve the best.

Chapter Three - Healing Takes Time
Prayer Journal

Be still and know that I am God. **Psalms 46:10a KJV**

1. How can you be still?

2. Sit in a very quiet space. No radio playing, no TV in the background, no one in the room (not even your cat or dog). Bring a pen and pad and set it beside you.

3. Now close your eyes and concentrate on your breathing. Clear your mind. If any important thought comes into your mind, jot it down on the pad so you can forget about it and go back to clearing your mind.

4. Remember you are not praying, you are not contemplating God, you are just sitting still. **This is very hard to do.**

5. If you are able to achieve this stillness this time, what did you hear? If you heard nothing, try again in an hour or so.

6. Could you hear your own breathing? Did you hear a car go down the street? Did you hear a bird? Can you recognize what type of bird? Did you hear a dog bark? Did you hear any machinery running in your house?

_____
_____
_____
_____

7. Go back and try to sit still again and see if you hear any of the things that were listed if you did not hear them before. Is there anything new that you noticed?

_____
_____
_____
_____

8. Did you smell anything? Cologne? Perfume? Cleaning fluid? Bathroom cleanser? Disinfectant? Soap? Shampoo? Hair Spray?

_____
_____
_____
_____

9. What might you become aware of next time you are still?

_____
_____
_____
_____

10. After you have cleared your mind of all thought, then ask God to speak to you. Maybe you will be able to "Know that He is God."

11. Now think about the following abilities. Next to each, list why it is special.

1. the sense of sight   - _____
2. the sense of hearing- _____
3. the sense of touch   - _____
4. the sense of taste   - _____
5. the sense of smell   - _____
6. the ability to laugh - _____
7. the ability to love   - _____

Scripture Reading

What are the special gifts that we are assured of in each of these different passages?

Lam. 3: 22-24

_____
_____
_____
_____

Psalms 23

_____
_____
_____
_____

Psalms 46: 9-11

_____
_____
_____
_____

NOTES

Section One
Time

Chapter Four
Give It Time

In this chapter, I want you to take a closer look at how you view yourself. Are you a whole human being when you are alone or only when you are part of a couple? I will give you a few examples of how our society has influenced how you think and then how it makes the process of healing a more difficult task than it really needs to be.

In many movies, from adult dramas to children's cartoons, a leading actor in a scene tells the supporting actor that they can't live without the other person, or that they need them to complete them in some way. Now that is a most flattering idea, that someone is not whole without you being part of his or her life, but is that really true? I want you to take a closer look at that statement and understand how our society has influenced you (mostly women) to think you can not exist without another person. You are not whole until you have found them and share your every moment with them.

Think back to your early childhood years. Something happened when you were a young infant. You will not even remember. The moment happened when you as a human being became autonomous. Autonomy is when you realize that you are independent, that you cause some things to happen and someone else causes other things to happen to or for you. At first, you didn't understand that when your tummy hurt that it was caused by your body and was not caused by someone else. Later, you began to realize the hunger pain was coming from within your body. You began to learn to pick up a toy, bat at a mobile above the crib, etc. You learned autonomy. You learned you were a separate human being and could do things by yourself. Eventuall,y you became so good at this you didn't want anyone else to do things for you or to you; you wanted to do it all by yourself. Because of autonomy, you fed and dressed yourself and were proud of it. You were created to develop in this way. You learned with time that you were an individual and you developed your personality. As you matured, your psyche was formed and was molded.

Through teen years, you became very self-conscious and sometimes your autonomy changed as you conformed in order to meet your strong need to belong. We want to love, to be loved, and to belong. So, sometimes you conform in order to have the sense of belonging, even though it is contradictory to your personality or nature, or even contrary to how your parents raised you to act.

Next, there is our society's influence and your autonomy takes yet another turn in the road. Before World War II in America, the vast majority of women were found only working in the home taking care of managing the home and rearing the children. During the war, many women worked jobs outside the home to help the war effort. When the war was over, many women returned to the home but many stayed in the paid work force. Some women had experienced their feelings of independence and autonomy, and found it difficult to return to a setting where someone else made the money and told them how to spend it. I am not saying this is bad or good. I am just giving an example of how feelings of autonomy are altered through many influences.

The main point is that you developed into an individual who is complete. You are complete as you are. You may have changed as you grew, but you will always be complete. God created you complete and made you a complement for others. Some believe He completes you by changing and forming your personality over time into the complete individual that He wants you to become in order that He can do a good work through you. This is stated:

6 Being confident of this very thing, that he which hath begun a good work in you will perform it until the day of Jesus Christ:
Philippians 1:6 (KJV)

Now, back to the original question. I want to ask you again, is this true? Can some human being complete you and are you incomplete without him or her? Before you say, "Hold on a minute. I want to be with someone. I don't want to be alone," it is okay to say that you do not want to be alone, but you need to realize that you need to view yourself as you were born to be - an autonomous, whole and complete individual.

A partner is a complement, similar to a condiment. The partner literally compliments you, praises you, affirms your ideas, and even helps you create new ideas during a brainstorming session therefore encouraging your growth and development. Now, if your partner left, the growth still took place and you are still complete. Your new growth may now come from within or without, but growth that has already taken place is still there.

Let us use another example with food. Think of yourself as a food item. You are complete in and of yourself. You are nourishing and have all the qualities necessary to be a good and healthy food. You can be consumed plain and really are tasty that way, too. Some people may like to be complemented with a condiment. It adds spice… the spice to life. The condiment is a want, but it is not a need. You will die if you do not get nourishment, yet you survive fine without the condiments.

The food can be complemented with many different condiments, making the original food quite different than the first way you experienced it. You may try the new condiment by accident. You were out of the usual one and thought you would try what you had on the shelf. Or, you were shopping in the store and found a new condiment at the grocery. You may find that the new condiment is superior to the first one, and if it hadn't been for the fact there was no more of the first condiment, you would not have found this superior one. Maybe your tastes have changed or maybe it was that you were never exposed to this new tasty option.

Remember the original food is good and nourishing just the way it came. You are complete and wonderful just the way you are. A partner is a complement, a condiment, a want, or a garnish. A partner is not a need, or someone that is meant to complete you. Persons in our lives complement us; sometimes it's a partner and sometimes they are your friends. You can't always get what you want, but you usually have all you need. Scripture puts it another way - God supplies your needs.

32b ...for your heavenly Father knoweth that ye have need of all these things. 33 But seek ye first the kingdom of God, and his righteousness; and all these things shall be added unto you.
Matthew 6:32b-33 (KJV)

The point is you don't always get what you want, but you are provided with what you truly need in this life, a whole autonomous psyche. Do not look for someone to complete you, but to complement you. In some wedding ceremonies, the two mothers of the bride and groom take lighted candles signifying their respective child's life and they light the large center candle signifying the joined married life. I have sometimes seen the individual candles blown out. They should not be, because they are not blown out in reality. The groom's and the bride's lives continue, but they burn brighter with the new marriage candle. When separation/divorce occurs, the center candle just goes out. The two separate candles burn on. Healing a broken heart when the complement has left takes time, but to heal you when you only have part of yourself because you are incomplete is near impossible. If the center candle went out and your individual candles were put out years ago, you would really be dead. You may feel you are not whole or are incomplete, but after you work through the exercises in this book and read new resources on the subject, you will feel more whole. Remember, you are a complete and wonderful person just the way you are. You have everything you need … You! And with time and God's help, you will heal and may be complemented again. **Give It Time**.

NOTES

Chapter Four – Give It Time
RESOURCES

Movies (dvd, tv, etc.)

Under the Tuscan Sun (2003)

Jerry Maguire (1996)

Songs

You Can't Always Get What You Want sung by The Rolling Stones

Books/Articles/Groups/Other Resources
(and articles on the internet)

Wright, H. Norman (2001). *Always Daddy's Girl*, Ventura: Regal Books. ISBN 0-8307-2762-0

Psychiatrists, Psychotherapists, and Psychologists

Robert Glaser, Ph.D.
Jean Piaget, Ph.D.

NOTES

Case Study #4

Merribelle was 46 years old. She had two grown children. She had a relatively happy life with her husband in the suburbs of a large city. Her husband worked for a large company making a very nice income. They had anything and everything they wanted. She did not work.

They had planned a vacation to give them some time together away from all other responsibilities. They had planned a Caribbean cruise with many amenities. They made reservations for an outside cabin with a terrace. They had booked their excursions in advance as well. They were going to lay around in the sun, enjoy the nice dinners and shows, and see some far away places.

The week before the cruise, Merribelle's husband of 25 years told her he was leaving and packed up and moved out. He had even gone to a lawyer and had separation papers prepared. He told her to keep the cruise, that he wasn't interested. Merribelle fell apart. She had no idea this was coming. She knew he had often worked late, golfed often, and spent little time at home for months. She cried for days. She asked her friends what she should do about the cruise. Travel insurance had not been purchased and she would not be able to get a refund. At the last moment, she decided she would still go. She mostly stayed in her large cabin and had room service bring her meals. She could not bear to sit at a table and have to admit that she was alone. She also wasn't very hungry.

It took much strength and an attitude of independence for Merribelle to go on the cruise. She was not enjoying it as she had originally planned, but she was acting "as if" she was emotionally strong and independent. Riding back on a transfer ferry after an excursion, she was sitting next to another woman who was alone. They began to talk, trading normal pleasantries. Then, Merribelle could not contain herself any longer and began to share the incident of her husband leaving her just a week before the cruise. The other woman then began to share her story of divorce and what she did to survive and heal from the heartbreak. Another woman who was sitting in the seat in front of Merribelle began to hear the conversation. When leaving the ferry to board the cruise ship, the third woman briefly agreed with the advice the second woman was giving Merribelle, because she had also gone through a divorce and found the same suggestions were what she had done during her healing time. She gave Merribelle hope when she introduced her to her new husband of two years.

The cruise did not cure Merribelle's heartbreak, but it did help her realize that she could do some things independently even if a condiment would have been much preferred. I would not recommend for you to go on a cruise alone, especially not at this stage of emotional distress, but I include this case study to illustrate autonomy, independence, and point out you are not alone. Many have gone through divorce and come out feeling whole again.

Chapter Four - Give It Time
Journal

In this chapter journal exercise, you are going to work on remembering your early childhood experiences. During this exercise, just reflect and don't feel. Act as if these experiences belong to someone else.

1. What is your earliest childhood memory? This may take some time to recall. First try to remember one that occurred early in your life...when you went to school. What was the day like? What school were you attending? What was your teacher's name? Who were the other children in your class? What happened? If you can't remember names, try to recall what they looked like. Please write the memory here. Try to write as much detail as possible.

2. Now, you will step back a little further in time. What is your first memory of you with your mother? What was the day like? Where were you? What happened? Please write this memory here. Remember to include as much detail as possible as if you are watching a movie of your life. Make note of your emotions here also, but remember to be the observer like the moviegoers who see the film and the great acting, but don't have to feel the emotion...the actors are doing it for you.

3. Now think about the memory you wrote. Was this from a photo in a family album where you heard the story so many times that you think you recall this. Has it been imprinted in your mind due to the photo and being told of the day? If this was a photographed happening with you and your mother, try to remember one that you recall where there is no photograph of the experience. How old were you? Who are all the characters in this scene? What happened that day? What were your feelings? Please write the memory here. Try to write as much detail as possible. (If #2 was not photographed and you recall a second experience, record that one here.)

4. Now, repeat the exercise with the following criteria: What is your first memory of you with your father? What was the day like? Where were you? What happened? Please write this memory here. Remember to include as much detail as possible as if you are watching a movie of your life. Make note of your emotions here also but remember to be the observer like the moviegoers who see the film and the great acting, but don't have to feel the emotion...the actors are doing it for you.

5. Do you have a second memory of you and your father that was also not photographed? Please write the memory here. Try to write as much detail as possible.

6. Do you have memories of you with your siblings? Record separately the earliest memories of you and each one of them. These do not need as much detail, just a note regarding each sibling.

7. If someone raised you other than your parents, repeat exercise 2-4 using the person(s) involved in your rearing. Be sure to make note of your feelings at the time. Of course, remember you are just watching a movie and actors and don't need to feel anything at this time. We don't want you to get bogged down with the emotions. Please write the memory here. Try to write as much detail as possible.

8. Now, take a deep breath. You have been traveling all over your memory. It has been loaded with emotions...possibly that is why you chose to place it in your memory in the first place. Refocus on where you are right now. You are not there anymore. You are here in your room.

What do you see?
_____

What do you hear?
_____

What do you smell?
_____

    I want to praise you. You have done some marvelous work today on moving forward in your life and picking up your pieces of a broken heart. Remember: **Healing Takes Time, Give It Time.**

    Note: If you did not do these exercises. Give It Time. Now that you know what I am asking you to recall, it will probably start coming back to you when you are not even working on it. When it does, I ask you to remember to record it here. You will be using these journal answers in later journal work. I thank you and you will thank yourself for having written something here when you get to that part of the book.

NOTES

Chapter Four – Give It Time
Prayer Journal

You have already been keeping your prayer journal in a separate little notebook. Of course, I do not want you to stop.

I want you to continue to remember specific others in your prayers each time you have completed your chapter journal exercises.

Thank the Lord for your unique personality and traits.

Thank the Lord specifically for each of the persons that you wrote about in your journal.

Ask the Lord to give you a clear mind to recall anything more that you should remember that would assist you at this time in your life.

Ask the Lord to help you through any painful memories that may have been unburied and for understanding of the purpose.

Thank the Lord for always being with you.

Thank the Lord for not being alone because the Lord is always with you and to be mindful that all you need to do is call upon Him.

Pray for God to remind you of your strengths.

List your strengths.

_____
_____
_____
_____
_____
_____
_____
_____
_____

Pray for God to remind you of your completeness.

List signs of your wholeness.

_____
_____

Scripture Reading

Read the following passages and note your thoughts.

Philippians 1:6

Matthew 6

Section One
Time

Chapter Five
Take the Time

In this chapter, I want you to realize that even though you would love this painful time to pass as quickly as possible, that it must progress at a healing pace. Healing our bodies may take place quickly on the surface, but it doesn't necessarily happen beneath the surface in the same amount of time. I am asking you to *Take the Time* to heal from the inside out.

An example that is similar to this is my dental experience at 33 years of age. I had three impacted wisdom teeth. They were extracted through dental surgery performed by a specialist, who stitched the areas. I returned a week later, to have the stitches removed. All looked fine, so off I went. Several nights later I awoke at 3 A.M. with pain that involved my entire lower jaw. It was so painful that I sat holding my jaw with my hands and rocking back and forth in hopes of soothing the pain. I did not call the dentist emergency line. I reasoned that it was normal and suffered on for almost a week. I was thinking my teeth were shifting now that they had the space available. Because of work and daytime distractions, I managed through the days but inevitably at 3 A.M. I would awake with the unbearable pain. I finally went back to the dentist and was told I had "dry sockets." The gums had healed on the surface, but inside had not. The nerves were being exposed to air and causing the pain. The dentist had to reopen the area and pack them with medicated gauze. I returned each week for new packing. I had the extractions in August, and at Thanksgiving was finally healed enough to remove all packing and let the surface area finish healing. My gums had to heal very slowly from the inside to the surface.

Through the journal exercises in Chapter 5, you will become aware of this type of healing. I want you to *Take the Time* with your *self* and look at the process of healing inside as well as outside. *Take the Time* to heal. When we were children, we thought that a band-aid had magic in it and once it was applied all was well. Also as children, the body healed faster because we were still growing and physical injuries could heal quickly. As we age, the ability to heal slows down. Now, as adults we know there is no magic band-aid. As adults we have learned procedures and remedies. We can even estimate the time it will take to heal and can evaluate the seriousness of an injury. We know when to try home remedies or over the counter medication. And we know when to seek professional help.

Ultimately, we are the ones responsible to set up the environment for healing. You can heal by setting up the environment for healing a broken heart caused by a broken relationship. If you feel so shattered that you can not set up the environment by yourself using self-help books, listening to speakers, and participating in groups, then seek the help of a professional in the field to guide you and take small steps back to a feeling of wellness. If you can take the responsibility for your own environment for emotional healing alone, read on.

In the last chapter, the journal work began with you remembering some of your important memories that helped form your view on life and persons in your life. Much of your adult views stem from these first opinions you formed. There is a problem with some of the opinions you formed, though. The problem with some of the opinions is that a child who hadn't experienced much of life formed them. Even though you grew to an adult size, you could still be having child size opinions.

Here is a child size opinion that I formed as a chil: I was 6 years old. My father took our dog and me with him to a field. He let the dog loose to run free. It began to get dark and the dog was no where in sight. He called for the dog multiple times, but the dog did not come or even bark in reply. He told me to stay near the car. He went looking for the dog. It took him forever. It got darker. I began to become fearful being alone in the dark in a place I had not been before. I had heard on TV about some man who was wanted for killing children. I began to think that maybe it was my dad. I was wondering if he was going to come back and even kill me. After about 10 minutes, he returned with the dog on the leash and we got in the car to return home. I never spoke of my feelings. I was glad that maybe my dad was not the killer. As an adult, when I think of this incident, I realize that he did not take me with him to get the dog due to the undergrowth of briars that were in the field. And I realize why he did not put me in the car - because I might have touched something sending the car rolling off. I realize I was such an obedient child that he knew I would stand there because he had said to stand there. I shared this memory with my dad a few years ago and told him my thoughts at the time. He said he had no idea that I would have been thinking such a horrible thing.

As an adult, I think that I would have picked me up and carried me when going to find the dog. Luckily, this childhood incident didn't have any lasting or harmful effect on my life, but it is one I remember vividly. It could have set my opinion in regard to my Dad to feel he was not to be trusted and would desert me. I did not form this view because years before I had set my opinion about him and nothing could shake it. I may be an adult in an adult body but I also carry around a child inside me that seems to never grow up. You may be an adult in an adult body but you also carry around a child inside of you that seems to never grow up. Like a movie, the memories are frozen at the age we were.

There are works by several psychologists about the "inner child." The Inner Child is a concept used in popular psychology to denote the childlike aspect of a person's psyche. Frequently, the term is used to address childhood experiences and the remaining effects. The inner child concept was popularized by the self-help movement. I highly recommend you read material on this topic. It is most beneficial and will go more into depth and do the subject and you credit. *Take The Time*.

    During my separation period, I saw a video on a TV station. This program motivated me to begin my healing from unwanted separation with the inevitable divorce on its way. The program was talking about the inner child and how you had to be responsible for that child now that you were an adult, take care of that child, and nurture that child within. That is when I realized that I had to be responsible for my little child. My parents were strong disciplinarians and I credit my morals to that training, but as a child I thought they were tougher on me than they needed to be. I felt at times unloved, even if I realized they did it because they did love me. So at this point, I cried for the little child in me and pledged to remember to take care of her. She belonged to me and I did not need to continue to be so hard on her. I needed to love her, take care of her, comfort her, and nurture her. This is what I want you to realize also. You have an inner child. Look for your inner child. What is your child trying to say to you? What is your child crying about? Cry with your child. This is where you set up the healing environment. You begin with your inner child. A lasting relationship needs to start with you and your inner child. Develop that relationship. Back in the 1970's there was a question spoken: "Who am I?" You may find that you can answer that question if you look to your inner child, as well as to your adult mind for a definitive explanation.

    You may have paused here contemplating your childhood, your upbringing, your memories, and the needs of your inner child. As you take responsibility for your inner child and "re-parent" your self, don't fall into wasting your emotional energy on blaming your parents, but direct your emotional energy toward loving and caring for you. Just forgive your parents their wrongs and let it go. You will probably not be able to ever forget the wrongs. As it is said, only God can forgive and then forget. That is divine; you are still human and you must be aware of your limitations and keep realistic expectations for yourself. You are going to "rewrite" the wrongs and "re-parent" your inner child in areas that need healing. You are going to hold to those memories that are positive and uplifting.

Look at several factors about your parents through your adult eyes. How old were your parents at the time of your memory? You may even have to do actual calculations to come up with this age. You will probably find that they were amazingly younger than you, the child, remembered them to be. When I was 24 years old, I thought I really was a knowledgeable adult that always made perfect decisions. When I looked at my son when he was that age, I realized how young I was at 24. I then realized that was how old my father was when I was born and my mother was 21. I then realized at 51 years of age that my parents were not old at all when I was born. It is understandable that they reared me the way they did. They were young, I was their first child, and they had little or no experience at parenting. My father's father had left him at age 6 and he didn't have even a father figure after which to model himself. They were doing their best.

If you take a good look at your parents and try to look at them through your adult eyes, you may find this to be true also. Look at your parents' role models and your parents' life stresses: economic problems, educational problems, mental problems, and physical problems. You can not change their problems. You can not change your childhood. You can change your perceptions, and your perceptions may be keeping old wounds festering up and never healing.

These inner child wounds can affect your relationship with others. You are demonstrating that you want to heal by reading this book. You have heard how Christ was the great physician; ask Him for help and strength as you work on the inner healing. The woman who touched Christ was seeking healing and was taking an active part in that healing. Notice Christ did not go to her, she came to Him. She had the desire to be healed and the faith that it would be done.

43 And a woman having an issue of blood twelve years, which had spent all her living upon physicians, neither could be healed of any,
44 Came behind him, and touched the border of his garment: and immediately her issue of blood stanched.
Luke 8:43-44 (KJV)

Begin the healing by treating yourself well. Don't spoil yourself. Reward yourself for your hard work on healing. Spoiling a child only creates a brat. Reward yourself for finding hurts from your childhood and then working on righting them: Rewriting and changing the perceptions of the memory.

Right the wrongs by studying, reflecting, and reading self-help literature. Analyze the Why's…why it hurts you, why you feel this way, why you need to help your inner child, etc. And discover your Wants…want to be loved, want to be cared for, want to be protected, want to feel safe, want to get what you want, want what you get, etc. In going deep you can heal the deep wounds, but remember, some deep healing needs a professional guiding you, not just some self-help book. The seriousness of the injury will dictate to you, the adult, that a professional is needed. If you are unsure, seek out a professional and get their opinion on your stability before you proceed. If you feel that you have been knocked down and had a good cry and that now you can get up and tend to the wound, then proceed.

Cuts heal best from the inside out, eventually getting to the surface. Remember, don't band aid the top surface wound without cleaning out the wound with antiseptic, promoting a good healing environment, leaving nothing inside to fester and become infected. Forgive those that may have been unknowingly mean to you, the child. Further into this book you may be able to forgive those who were knowingly mean to you, the child. You have heard the term "cut your losses." If it is impossible to forgive, then you may have to do just that in regard to these issues. Just pick up where you are and take your inner child by the hand and begin to LOVE that child. You deserve to be loved, nurtured, embraced, protected, and treated with tenderness. **Take the Time**.

NOTES

Chapter Five – Take The Time
RESOURCES

Movies (dvd, tv, etc.)

Bradshaw, John. *Homecoming, Reclaiming Your Inner Child*

Songs

Treasure of You, sung by Steven Curtis Chapman on the Heaven in the Real World album.

Books/Articles/Groups/Other Resources
(and articles on the internet)

Harris, Thomas Anthony (1969). *I'm OK, You're OK,* Harper & Row. ISBN 0-380-00772-X

Smith, Blaine (January 2004). *Reshaping Assumptions That Shape Our Life*, Nehemiah Ministries.

Psychiatrists, Psychotherapists, and Psychologists

Eric Berne
Carl Jung
Emmet Fox
Charles Whitfield

NOTES

Case Study #5

Gary was 39 years old. He had been married twice. His first marriage ended after two years. Reflecting back on those years, he felt he was too young and did not apply himself to the marriage. His wife left him for another man who had been his friend.

After two years of being alone, he decided he needed to get out and find some way to meet someone again. This was the 70's; he signed up for dance classes and started going to dance clubs. The instructors at the dance studio introduced him to another student. They began dating and ended up marrying.

It lasted 13 years. They seemed well suited for each other, even though they had their differences. During these years, they underwent various changes in jobs, schooling, and places to live. They grew together as a couple facing the many challenges. They had developed many friends.

One day his wife said she had started seeing another man and she did not intend for it to happen, but she had fallen in love with him. She did not even try to hide it from Gary. She even pushed Gary to the point of asking, what was he going to do about it. One of their closest friends invited them to their place for a weekend. The man counseled Gary all weekend while the woman talked with Gary's wife. Unfortunately, it did not change anything and finally they separated and divorced. Around the same time, he had lost his job and was devastated by the rejection.

He enrolled in a university for training in a new field. The course work would take him two years to complete as he was going through the divorce proceedings. One day while walking across campus after a class, he actually collapsed on the sidewalk. He lay there for several minutes, just trying to find energy to pick himself up. He was emotionally drained. He did get up and then decided he could not go on this way alone. He needed professional help to give him strategies for coping with his emotions and the loss.

Gary gives credit to individual counseling and attending divorce and separation group meetings for his recovery. He says it was the lowest point in his life and sometimes wonders how he got through it.

NOTES

Chapter Five – Take The Time
Journal

In this chapter journal exercise you are going to work on evaluating through an adult's eyes your early childhood experiences. This adult evaluating of childhood experiences is called "rewriting." During this journal exercise, remember to just reflect and don't invoke the old feelings. I don't want you to remove the scab that is on your wound; I want you to put a special medicated ointment on it that is made to eliminate the chance of permanent scarring. So remember to act as if these experiences belong to someone else.

1. First, read your earliest childhood memory that you wrote about in the Chapter 4 Journal. Place yourself into the experience as an adult observer. Rewrite the experience here without any emotion or feelings. Tell what happened, but not how it felt. Try to place yourself in the shoes of the adult, evaluate the adult's actions. As the adult what do you think your motives were? Since you were a child, you reacted as a child. Observing the experience now as a grown adult, how do you think an adult would have reacted if this were happening to them and not a child. What would the adult "child" do or say?

_____
_____
_____
_____
_____
_____
_____
_____
_____
_____
_____
_____
_____
_____
_____
_____
_____
_____
_____

2. Take a look at one of your first memories of you with your mother that you wrote about in the Chapter 4 Journal. Place yourself into the experience as an adult observer. Rewrite the experience here without any emotion or feelings. Tell what happened but not how it felt. Place yourself in the shoes of your

mother. Evaluate her actions. As a mother (note: not your mother, just a mother) what do you think your motives were? Since you were a child, you responded in this experience as a child. Observing the experience now as a grown adult, how do you think an adult would have reacted if this were happening to the adult and not a child. What would the adult "child" do or say?

_____
_____
_____
_____
_____
_____
_____
_____
_____
_____
_____
_____
_____
_____
_____
_____
_____
_____
_____
_____

3. Take a look at one of your first memories of you with your father that you wrote about in the Chapter 4 Journal. Place yourself into the experience as an adult observer. Rewrite the experience here without any emotion or feelings. Tell what happened but not how it felt. Place yourself in the shoes of your father. Evaluate his actions. As a father (note: not your father, just a father) what do you think your motives were? Since you were a child, you responded in this experience as a child. Observing the experience now as a grown adult, how do you think an adult would have reacted if this were happening to the adult and not a child. What would the adult "child" do or say?

_____
_____
_____
_____
_____
_____

4. Do you have memories of you with your siblings? Record separately the earliest memories of you and each one of them. These do not need as much detail, just a note regarding each sibling.

5. If someone raised you other than your parents, repeat exercise 2-4 using the person(s) involved in your rearing. Be sure to make note of your feelings at the time. Of course, remember you are just watching a movie and actors and don't need to feel anything at this time. I don't want you to get bogged down with the emotions. Please write the memory here. Try to write as much detail as possible.

_____
_____
_____
_____

6. Refocus on where you are right now. You are not there any more. You are here in your room.

   What do you see?
   _____

   What do you hear?
   _____

   What do you smell?
   _____

     I want to praise you. You have done some marvelous work today on moving forward in your life and picking up your pieces of a broken heart. Remember: **Healing Takes Time, Give It Time, and Take The Time.**

Note: If you did not do these exercises, *Take The Time*. It may be because you did not do the journal in Chapter 4. I ask you to record your memories now in Chapter 4 and then come back to this journal on the next day and complete it. I thank you and you can thank yourself for taking the time to heal from the inside out.

Chapter Five – Take The Time
Prayer Journal

Recall the first time you can remember thinking about God. How old were you? Remember that the "inner child" that we take with us has the necessary ingredient that makes it easier to see the kingdom of God.

Pray giving thanks and taking your supplications before Almighty God.

Let your inner child gaze on the beauty of the kingdom of God and remember who is OUR Father and how much He loves us.

Please Take The Time to be with the Lord. He wants to hear from you and He wants to speak to you and touch your heart.

After taking this prayer time, reflect on the paragraph below. Think about what you will do today to improve your mindset.

Remember happiness is something that happens when you decide to be happy ahead of time. You determine happiness. The older you get, the more you realize how many things in life are not perfect and how grateful you really are for the simplest things that can bring you joy. Memories sometime can bring you pain, but then some memories can bring you joy. Be mindful of the things that can steal this joy. Free yourself of worries and hatred. Make your life as simplistic as possible. Expect less out of life in general and give more positive thought and energy to creating an environment that brings you peace and joy.

Scripture Reading
Read the following passages and note your thoughts.

Philippians 4:4-7

_____

_____

Colossians 1:11-13

_____

_____

What can you do today about joy?

_____
_____

Section One
Time

Chapter Six
Take A Long Time

At this point, you have taken time to heal. You have done this by working on your inner self through taking advantage of the journal exercises and by following the guided prayer journal exercises at the end of each chapter. And time has been on your side. Remember to continue to *Take A Long Time* to heal while you use these tools to help yourself. I believe you will continue to find them helpful, as you become stronger.

The subject of this chapter will be taking one last look back. This is sometimes called "giving it a last chance" or "the point of no return." I am going to direct you in taking a long, clear look at your marriage and in considering moving on carefully. In the prior chapters, you have addressed healing and giving yourself time to do so. Now that the hurts or inner wounds are not as fresh as they were when the separation began, it is easier to take the long look back without emotionally falling apart and/or literally physically collapsing.

The long, clear look that I am talking about is truly evaluating the possibility of reconciliation. By definition, the word reconciliation means the process of making consistent or compatible. I want you to think about the word consistent. The healing work you have been doing has been making your building blocks consistent and, therefore, strengthening you. The work also has been making you a person who can be more compatible. Yet, from a legal way of thinking, the word reconciliation means a compatibility and consistency in marriage or in a relationship. When someone is talking about reconciliation, they usually mean going back or getting back together. Before I write more about this part of the definition, I want you to remember the story of the Israelites according to the Old Testament.

In the book of Exodus, the Israelites had left exile and slavery in Egypt and had crossed over the Red Sea after a series of miracles that were performed by God. They were being fed manna from heaven each day and they had fresh water when they needed it. God, through Moses, told the Israelites that they were going into a land that flowed with "milk and honey." By the book of Numbers, they began to complain about the manna and wanted meat, and were saying that they were better off in Egypt. At least in Egypt they had meat, cucumbers, and melons.

4 And the mixt multitude that was among them fell a lusting: and the children of Israel also wept again, and said, Who shall give us flesh to eat?
5 We remember the fish, which we did eat in Egypt freely; the cucumbers, and the melons, and the leeks, and the onions, and the garlick:
6 But now our soul is dried away: there is nothing at all, beside this manna, before our eyes.

31 And there went forth a wind from the LORD, and brought quails from the sea, and let them fall by the camp, as it were a day's journey on this side, and as it were a day's journey on the other side, round about the camp, and as it were two cubits high upon the face of the earth.
32 And the people stood up all that day, and all that night, and all the next day, and they gathered the quails: he that gathered least gathered ten homers: and they spread them all abroad for themselves round about the camp.
33 And while the flesh was yet between their teeth, ere it was chewed, the wrath of the LORD was kindled against the people, and the LORD smote the people with a very great plague.
34 And he called the name of that place Kibrothhattaavah: because there they buried the people that lusted.
Numbers 11: 4-6, 31-34 (KJV)

Then later in the story, they were ready to go into the "promised" land but they decided to send in a reconnaissance team of spies to see what the people and place looked like. They were having their doubts even before the team brought back the report. When they did get the reports, they chose to hear what they wanted to hear.

1 And all the congregation lifted up their voice, and cried; and the people wept that night.
2 And all the children of Israel murmured against Moses and against Aaron: and the whole congregation said unto them, Would God that we had died in the land of Egypt! or would God we had died in this wilderness!
3 And wherefore hath the LORD brought us unto this land, to fall by the sword, that our wives and our children should be a prey? were it not better for us to return into Egypt?
4 And they said one to another, Let us make a captain, and let us return into Egypt.

20 And the LORD said, I have pardoned according to thy word: 21 But as truly as I live, all the earth shall be filled with the glory of the LORD.
22 Because all those men which have seen my glory, and my miracles, which I did in Egypt and in the wilderness, and have tempted me now these ten times, and have not hearkened to my voice;
23 Surely they shall not see the land which I sware unto their fathers, neither shall any of them that provoked me see it:
24 But my servant Caleb, because he had another spirit with him, and hath followed me fully, him will I bring into the land whereinto he went; and his seed shall possess it.
25 (Now the Amalekites and the Canaanites dwelt in the valley.) Tomorrow turn you, and get you into the wilderness by the way of the Red sea.
Numbers 14:1-4, 20-25 (KJV)

I am asking you to send in your reconnaissance team so to speak. The team consists of you and your spouse. Are the two of you on speaking terms at all? Can you speak to each other without yelling and losing your temper? Do you feel you can forgive your spouse for the cause of the separation? I know you may still hold resentments, anger, and pain, but is there a possibility of forgiveness that would be necessary to go back? Would you even be able to sit in the same room with your spouse and talk over the issues leading to the separation? Would you be able to now voice your real feelings?

Of course, I would not want you to do any of these things without the aid of a professional to assist and guide the two of you through such discussions. This book is written not for the purpose of being a reconciliation tool, but as a tool to help persons going through the pain of separation and divorce.

The purpose of the story of the Israelites is so you can see the price that is paid for not following God all the way. They were shown signs and wonders, yet several times they ignored those and cried for something else. Some were struck dead, or with disease, and others were left to wander in the desert for 40 years. You do not want to be still in this emotionally weak predicament for 40 years. You want to live the abundant life.

So what am I saying? I am saying, "Go to God's Promised Land!" Honor commitments and ask to always follow His will. It might mean moving forward and divorce, or it might mean reconciliation. I know you are thinking those two ideas are opposing each other - how can they both be honoring God and your commitments? Maybe, like the Israelites, you were being set free. Set free of abuse, a relationship filled with infidelity, or a marriage filled with addictions. In those and other cases, God may have been setting you free and wants a commitment from you to trust Him to carry you to the promised land and a better way of life. God does want a good and holy life for His children. In other cases, God has given you *both* time to be separate and be strengthened while being alone with Him and is ready for you to go back and live by the commitments you voiced together the day you said your vows to each other. Only you and your spouse know. Only the two of you know for sure. I believe you know the answer to the reconciliation question if you have searched your heart and spent time in prayer. Are there two?

Now let me address reconciliation a little more, in case you have decided that is an option for you. If you have decided it is not, then jump forward to the journal work. For the rest of you, I want you to consider the word reconciliation. I want you to break it down into syllables of sounds.

1) Recon 2) Cili 3) A 4)Tion

1) Recon

RECON is a mission to gather information to determine what method of approach to take. Also don't forget to <u>recogn</u>ize the reasons, the faults, and all the circumstances leading to your separation in the first place. Remember, if you choose reconciliation you both will need marriage counseling (therapy) if as a couple the two of you are going to reconcile for keeps. You will have many RECON sessions with the marriage counselor before you should consider living a life together.

2) Cili

Don't be <u>silly</u> and return because it would be easier or cheaper, or a multitude of silly excuses to resume a marriage that isn't all it is supposed to be.

3) A (B C's)

A- <u>Analyze</u> where you have brought yourself
B- <u>Be</u> kind
C- <u>See</u> things with your eyes and not your heart.
D- Don't let your heart be <u>Dead.</u>
E- <u>Engage</u> in true communication even if it means there is no hope of reconciliation in the end.

4)Tion

Don't <u>Shun</u> your original commitment before God and man IF an inner voice is speaking to BOTH of you saying "Love is STILL here" and " Time has healed both of your hurts" that caused the separation. Don't shun your responsibilities to give the marriage all your effort with professional help.

You have to analyze your mistakes and determine what you both did wrong; you have to identify what you both can do differently next time; and learn from your failure. You can work through your mistakes so that you both can move forward through reconciliation or eventually to divorce if that ends up ultimately the case.

This decision is all yours and of course, your spouse's. If it were all yours, then it can't and won't happen. As was said before, it takes two. Stop looking back and wanting "the meat and cantaloupes" and start looking forward to the "milk and honey." You are at the point of no return; say goodbye to yesterday and turn to face the new day.

Complete the journal and take time to use the prayer journal. These tools are included in the book to help you on your journey to your new abundant life. They have been included to help gird you up and make you strong as you face your life and its situations and circumstances. Take full advantage of them as you **Take A Long Time** on your inner self. Remember, you deserve the best. Give it to yourself because only you can truly do it. Take the time. **Take A Long Time**.

Chapter Six – A Long Time
RESOURCES

Movies (dvd, tv, etc.)

Osteen, Joel. *Developing a Habit of Happiness,* Broadcast #310 Joel Osteen Ministries, www.joelosteen.com .

Songs

It Takes Two written by Sylvia Moy and William Stevenson.
Love and Learn sung by Steven Curtis Chapman

Books/Articles/Groups/Other Resources
(and articles on the internet)

Mayer, Jeffry (1998). *Success is a Journey: 7 Steps to Achieving Success in the Business of Life,* New York: McGraw – Hill.
ISBN 0070411298

Psychiatrists, Psychotherapists, and Psychologists

Carl Rogers
Rollo May

NOTES

Case Study #6

Patricia was raised in a church. Her father was a deacon. She graduated from college and taught school. A new pastor had begun service at her family church. The new pastor had an adult son. Patricia met the pastor's son and after dating, fell in love and was married.

Patricia was active in her church and gave of her time to support various programs. She taught children's Sunday school classes as well as served on various committees. Growing up, she saw her father actively involved in church. She thought since her husband's father was a pastor he would have been raised in a similar vein of thought. Her husband seemed to not be as involved, and from the congregation's way of thinking, he did not attend much. Everyone thought " Oh! He's a Preacher's Kid," meaning rebellious and deliberately shunning religion. The congregation figured in time he would grow out of his ways and all would be well.

Eventually, Patricia stopped attending and serving. Years passed by. There was a small church nearby that opened. Patricia began attending and began teaching again. Her husband at first attended and looked as if he had turned over a new leaf. But with time, they separated. Then the true story came out. The husband had addiction problems and the first time they stopped attending was due to the severity of his addiction. Then they began attending local support group meetings and found other couples in similar situations. They even went for marriage counseling. Because the husband was staying clean of his problems, they began attending church together. Because Patricia was hopeful, she began getting back to her way of life, being involved in serving.

Unfortunately, her husband could not stay substance free and separation resulted. Some people did not think she had been a good wife and that she did not honor her commitment, and even put the blame on her, thinking that certainly a preacher's son wouldn't ever divorce. But as time passed, the information eventually leaked out.

Patricia found other Christians who had gone through divorce and began getting support from them. She found she didn't have to live a life in secret any longer. She also knew she had done all she could by supporting her husband through recovery and marriage counseling, so when they eventually divorced it was not because she had not given it her best.

NOTES

Chapter Six – Take A Long Time
Journal

In the prior chapters' journal exercises you have worked on your early childhood experiences. Now it is time to begin to evaluate some of your adult experiences. Still, in this journal exercise remember to just reflect and don't invoke the old feelings. So remember to act as if these experiences belong to someone else.

List below all the feelings you have regarding your spouse and the separation. Then, next to the feeling, list the reason you have for the emotion.

1. _____ -

2. _____ -

3. _____ -

4. _____ -

5. _____ -

List anything you consider that you did wrong to hurt the marriage?
Explain what you could have done instead in that case to strengthen the marriage.

1._____-   _____
                       _____
                       _____

2._____-   _____
                       _____
                       _____

3._____-   _____
                       _____
                       _____

4._____-   _____
                       _____
                       _____

List what your spouse did that you consider wrong and what the spouse could have done to correct it.

1._____-   _____
                       _____
                       _____

2._____-   _____
                       _____
                       _____

3._____-   _____
                       _____
                       _____

4._____-   _____
                       _____
                       _____

Now, I want you to take this list to the prayer journal in this chapter and go through the exercise there and work through the forgiveness of yourself and your spouse, so that you can free yourself from blaming yourself or your spouse. Pointing blame is not a step in healing. Identifying the area and forgiving the error will help you to move on to a better life. Free from blame, shame, and permanent injury. You may have never used the prayer journal in this book. It does not mean you can not benefit from some of the exercises there. Please at least read the exercises over in each and consider their value in helping you. Remember to **Take A Long Time**, because you are worth it.

NOTES

Chapter Six – Take A Long Time Prayer Journal

Release In Love Exercise

Take some of your memories dealing with your separation and marriage and practice this exercise with several different events. Before you begin, ask for God's help. Ask for His love, His comfort, and His guidance. Thank Him for His strength that He promises us.

Now take an event and pass through each of the following steps.

See It (Coming To Mind)

Let It In

Experience It (while staying above it)

Analyze the Effect

Work on Healing (breath in the balm and breath out the pain)

Let it Out

Release It in Love!

Repeat the exercise using several events. This works for those moving forward with divorce and those moving forward to reconciliation. The painful memories need to be released in love. Harboring them only hurt us more in the end.

Remember to magnify your God and not your problem. Let God help you with your problem. By using this exercise, you are magnifying your God who can help you let go of the unhappiness, so that you can make room for the happiness to come.

Scripture Reading

Read the story of the Israelites starting in Exodus at the parting and crossing of the Red Sea (Ex. 14:16-31) and then read where they were crossing the Jordan River (Josh. 3: 5-17)

1. What similarities are there between the two crossings?

2. What significance does this story hold in your life? What reassurance can you take from those experiences?

Read Joshua 1:9

Section One
Time

Chapter Seven
Take A Really Long Time

In the last chapter, you recognized the point of no return. This chapter will be moving past it. You will be making a transition where you *Take A Really Long Time,* closing one door and then begin to open the new one. In this chapter, I am going to direct your attention to the stages of loss or death. Basically, divorce affects us emotionally the same way a death would. The exception is that the undead (the ex) can truly revisit us and sometimes, when we least expect it, catch us unaware and not equipped to handle it, even after years have passed. When this reaction does occur, it helps us to see that some issue that we thought we dealt with is not completely finished and needs a little more exploring. It is normal for it to *Take A Really Long Time*.

Some of you were actually abandoned physically as well as emotionally. There are stages of abandonment that are similar in some ways to the stages of death that I will cover in more depth later. Abandonment can cause an emotional shattering and withdrawal. You internalize and as time goes on rage develops as a result of the hurt. Over time as you recover, a lifting of your spirit comes again. I think you will see that this is similar to the stages of death that I am going to spend more time on. Please remember to do your own research on topics as I cover them. Go to the internet, or your local bookstore self-help shelf, and find new resources that can also meet your needs.

The stages of death were written about in the late 60's. As I have said before, it has been explored by many since. On the internet I found there was one site that even had 7 stages listed. I first received a booklet on the subject from my pastor when I had spoken with him about my own separation in the 90's and then I was given another form of the stages when attending a seminar for separated and divorced people. The point that is always made about these stages is that it is not like a course or recipe where you proceed in a preordained order of 1, then 2, then 3 and so forth and voila you are done. These stages exist and you may have moved through them and then next you know, you are back where you started. I don't want to leave you without hope, though. If you have been working through this book at a slow and thorough pace, then time and God has helped you with the healing process. It is always good to know and understand that what you have and will be going through is normal and to be expected.

The five stages of loss that I will be using, as they relate to separation and divorce, are 1) Denial 2) Anger 3) Bargaining 4) Grief or Depression and 5) Acceptance. On a seven stage version I mentioned, there was shock and guilt added as two extra stages. Usually, shock is included with denial and guilt sometimes is associated with anger. I will begin to explain how each of these stages relates to your separation and divorce.

First, Denial is a normal reaction to the reality of the situation. It is normal to rationalize emotions that are too overwhelming for us to deal with. Denial is often what you do when the shock is too much to take. It acts as a defense mechanism to protect you from the pain. When I first attended the seminar, I thought that I actually was at the stage of acceptance. I could not understand how others, that had separated a year before, could still be in the stage of depression. In looking back now, I realize I was in the stage of denial.

A second stage is Anger. Strong emotions may be expressed as anger and be aimed at family, friends, strangers or even objects. Strong resentments may be expressed due to your spouse causing you such pain in leaving you and making you feel so isolated. Afterwards, you may even feel guilt for feeling anger. You become angry for feeling guilty for feeling angry. Unlike death, you often do rightfully blame your spouse for leaving you.

The third stage is Bargaining. A normal reaction to feelings of vulnerability and helplessness is expressed in a need to regain control of your life. You start second-guessing yourself. If only you had done something better (dressed better, cleaned better, cooked better, looked better), or if only we had gone here or there (on vacation, out to dinner more or out less, to events more together) or if only we had gone to marriage counseling years ago. All the "only if …then we would be happily together" statements are examples of the bargaining stage. Sometimes you might have even experienced this stage by bargaining with God.

A fourth stage is Depression. You are obviously aware of this stage. Sadness is expressed due to the loss of the marriage and regret that any of this ever had to take place. Then there are the feelings of separation and isolation as you pack away objects that remind you of times in the marriage when things were different, or at least when you were happily unaware anything was wrong. This is sometimes called the slippery slope. Just when you think you are climbing out of depression, you catch yourselves sliding back in again. Reassurance and hugs certainly can help you through these times.

The last stage is Acceptance. This does not mean that this stage is filled with happiness. Yet, it is not depression either. It is a stage where you now realize the separation and/or divorce is a fact and you are beyond the anger and denial. Not that you are at peace with it, but that you are ready to face the fact that life moves on and that includes yours. It is a realization that you are ready to move on.

Now, how does separation/divorce differ from death? Well, obviously your spouse isn't dead even if you wished they were. And because of this factor, you can have visitations. Usually a "visitation" is speaking of a ghost or spirit visiting you. The similarity in the separated and divorced person's life is that it can be as frightening as a real ghostly visitation. Think of it this way: your spouse is a symbol of what once was. The symbol or ghost is just a reminder of the marriage that is now dead, but this ghost is not really the marriage.

It took two of you to breathe life into the marriage and give it your blood (energy, time, romance, and love). When one stops and/or two stop, there is no longer life. The life form called "marriage" no longer exists – no longer lives. It must be buried or it will just rot and fester and smell. (It is time to bury the hatchet that killed it, also.) But that takes time and acceptance. You must realize the marriage called "The Jones" (or whatever your last name was) is not coming back. So, all the things you could positively or negatively do will not bring back its life.

Look at the list below and see how these are just forms of bargaining. Do you really want to enliven something dead? Make a zombie in its place – it walks, it talks, but it is no longer truly alive. It just goes through motions but blood doesn't really come from the heart due to the damage done. The cut was too deep. All of the life force is gone.

<u>Positive</u>
Understanding – seeing the issues, the different sides
Taking responsibility for your wrongs
Forgiving their wrongs
Listing why you feel in love with your spouse
Thinking of ways to support things you loved about your spouse
Loving yourself and improving yourself because of it
Loving your spouse more because you love you more

<u>Negative</u>
Complaining
Criticizing
Crying
Yelling
Gossiping
Shaming
Belittling
Judging
Punishing

Why would someone want to make a zombie marriage anyway? The following are some reasons that have been used before to send sparks through the body of marriage to sustain its life a little longer:

<u>Reasons for Making Zombies</u>

1. For the Kids – until they get …

    Through high school
    Through college
    Out of college
    On their own
    Have a solid career
    Married
    Established

2. For the Economy – 2 incomes pay for everything you share
    The house
    The cars
    The way of life
    The health care

3. For Social Reasons

    The friends
    The family
    The church
    The association
    The employer

Before the Vietnam War Era, there were zombie marriages, or at least that is how some marriages were. That is, except for the perfect ones portrayed on television. Real marriages were sometimes similar to arranged marriages. After the presence of the "Love Generation," people felt marriage should include love, trust, companionship, and a host of other attributes. Today, people speak of finding their "soul mates" and divorce is spoken of in normal conversations. There are no longer "broken homes." We have learned in American society that we all live in glass houses and don't throw stones. We have realized that we live in these glass houses so nothing is really a secret. The more we try to hide, the worse it is for us as we live our lives. Persons have learned from their mistakes, picked up the pieces and moved on, and the next marriage has benefited from the mistakes of the prior marriage. But some of those have failed again, because they have not learned to work on the one marriage partner (themselves) while they have the time. They have rushed into a new marriage and forgotten to throw out the baggage from the past, or to bury the old garbage, and they are stinking up the new marriage. This often has caused new rot and inevitable death to the next marriage due to the infection.

So, Where do you go from here? What can you do? Move forward and don't resurrect the past, but reframe it. Look at it a different way. Change some of the terminology you use that keeps you from letting go of it.

There is an interesting strategy that is called NeuroLinguistic Programming (NLP). Through NLP exercises you can alter the way you think and feel regarding the past which may be negatively affecting you and preventing you from moving forward in a constructive way.

I will be directing you later using some exercises that relate to your positive intentions and behaviors. At this point, I am asking you to just review each of the presuppositions of NLP and try them on for size. You can find them on the internet. Sometimes, you have supposed some things to be true regarding yourselves and how you view and deal with others in life. Those suppositions have kept you from obtaining greater things in life. Since you are moving forward to a more abundant life, I want you to begin to rethink those suppositions and see how you can be free of some of the bonds that hold you back. Put very simply, I have found NLP teaches you how to approach reality and how to search for answers from within your *self*. I first experienced NLP when invited by a friend to attend a weekend seminar conducted by Richard McHugh, S.J., Ph. D. He used the techniques to benefit individuals with their personal life issues. I found the exercises and his techniques of guidance to be marvelous. He published a book of exercises called "Mind with A Heart, creative patterns of personal change." If you can find it in print, you will find it well worth getting. If you select serious events to use in each exercise, you will have meaningful and life changing results.

When you finish the journal and prayer journal exercises of Chapter 7, you will have truly completed beneficial work and should congratulate your *self* for **Taking A Really Long Time** because *It's All About Time*. A broken heart heals in time with love and tenderness. The next and second section of the book will be devoted to what you have been looking for, - Love.

NOTES

Chapter Seven – A Really Long Time
RESOURCES

Movies (dvd, tv, etc.)
Dinner With Friends (2001)

Songs
Time, Love, and Tenderness written and sung by Michael Bolton

Books/Articles/Groups/Other Resources
(and articles on the internet)
Kubler-Ross, Elsabeth (1969). On Death and Dying. NY: Touchstone ISBN 0-684-83938-5

McHugh, Richard P. (1998). Mind With A Heart. Gujarat Sahitya Prakash, India.

Satir, Virginia (1975). *Self Esteem.* Berkely, CA: Celestial Arts. ISBN 1-58761-094-9.

Bandler, Richard, John Grinder & Virginia Satir (1976). *Changing with Families: a book about further education for being human.* Palo Alto, CA: Science & Behavior Books. ISBN 0-8314-0051-X.

NLP on the Web *www.rain.org/~da5e/nlpfaq.html*
          www.nlp.com

Psychiatrists, Psychotherapists, and Psychologists

Fritz Perls (Gestalt Therapy)
Milton Erickson
Virginia Satir

NOTES

Case Study #7

Jacqueline was in her forties and was married for 18 years. They had two sons, one in high school and the other in junior high. She and her husband had their own business and worked together as a team. They made presentations of their product every weekend. Their customers followed the company dealings closely. Even their two sons were in the limelight, but not directly in the process of the sales.

One weekend while setting up for the presentation, Jacqueline was speaking with one of their regular customers. This customer was telling her how she thought it was so nice how her husband treated her like a lady even when no one was watching. Of course, this peaked Jacqueline's interest and she asked exactly what did she mean. The customer then told her how she had seen her and her husband leaving a restaurant that week. And how he had opened the car door for her and had made sure her dress was in the car before shutting the door. Jacqueline knew this had not been her but continued to gather information from the customer thinking she could help the customer eventually see it was not she and her husband, without making him not seem to be the gentleman that she thought he was. Jacqueline asked her about the car's description since her husband's business car was quite recognizable with their logo boldly painted on its side. The customer was not mistaken; it had been the husband and the car, yet it had not been Jacqueline, since she had been out of town all week at a special conference.

Jacqueline then excused herself and went to find the husband to confront him. Confront him she did, but she did not get the reaction that she thought she would get. Instead of saying he was sorry, it was a mistake, or it was misinterpreted, or a million of other excuses, he said just the opposite. He told her they could stay together, he could continue the affair and they could keep the business going. And if she didn't like it and she made a big deal out of it in front of their clients, he would take her down, too. The business would be over and their comfortable lifestyle would drastically change for the worse.

Jacqueline chose to make a big deal of it right before the customers. And the business closed that day with all the clients in shock at the display of dirty laundry instead of the usual product that they had all come to trust and depend on. Sadly, this is also how the two sons were told of their parents' immediate separation.

Jacqueline could have waited for the presentation to be over and been more maternal and protected her sons from the public display of emotions. She certainly had a right to be upset; yet everyone else did not have to be involved in her drama. The world was not her living room, bedroom or lawyer's office.

Chapter Seven – Take A Really Long Time
Journal

In the prior chapters' journal exercises, I have asked you to act as if these experiences belong to someone else. Today's journal is going to be different. I want you to totally be with it emotionally. I want you to fully feel it. I want you to set a stage to remember this was your turning point after taking a really long time mending your heart.

The exercise you are going to engage in with this journal is going to take your creativity. I want you to invest the time and fully participate in this exercise. I want you to plan a funeral. Yes, you read it right. I want you to plan and participate in a funeral. Who are you burying? You will be burying your marriage. It has died and you have agreed that there was no turning back at the end of Chapter Six "Take a Long Time." So that means the marriage is officially dead and gone, and a funeral or memorial service is in order. Think about how real funerals or memorial services are conducted. Use them as models for the funeral service you will plan. I want you to physically participate in the service, but I am not suggesting you invite anyone to the service. This is a very private service for the benefit of your *self*. It is not for you and your friends, and it is not to be done in mockery and jest. I really want you to officially bury the past and the marriage and shed tears and then turn and move forward with your new life. So now that is all explained, get started on the plans.

Arrangements must be made.

1. What box will you use for the casket?

_____
_____

2. How will you decorate this box, turning it into the casket?

_____
_____
_____
_____

3. What <u>copies </u>of articles will you place in the casket to be symbols of the marriage? (Note that I say copies; do not use the real objects. One suggestion may be a *copy* of your marriage license. You need to keep the real license because in some cases it may be required.)

What other suggestions can you think of?

_____
_____

4. What words will you say as a eulogy to memorialize the good years of the marriage?

_____
_____
_____
_____

(You may need to use a separate piece of paper to write a proper eulogy.)

5. What music will you use?

_____

6. Which pictures will you choose to set by the casket?

_____

7. What date will you choose to perform the service?

_____

Now that you have decided on the arrangements, go about actually preparing everything for the day you will hold the private service. Remember you are performing this service because you truly grieve for the loss of a marriage and possibly some good memories. Even though the marriage has died, the good memories never have to change or be buried. They just will not be brought out and looked at as often. In time, they may even become memories that are hard to believe really happened in your life, yet there are pictures or letters and cards to prove it.

Physically perform the funeral/memorial service. Use the music, speak the eulogy, dig a hole, bury the box, cry your tears and respectfully walk away.

After performing the service, describe the emotions you felt and explain why you felt that way.

_____
_____
_____
_____

Chapter Seven – Take A Really Long Time
Prayer Journal

Begin by praying and thanking God for how far you have come since the first day of separation. Ask for His continued guidance, healing power and strength. Be mindful of all the good things happening in your life. Be still and listen to Him. Close your prayer in thanks and praise.

Read Job 42:7-17.

1. How did God renew Job's life when all his old life was gone?

_____
_____
_____
_____

2. What hope can you draw from the story of Job?

_____
_____
_____
_____

Think about the famous poem Footprints in the Sand. Are you being carried right now or are you more like the poem related to Broken Dreams where you have asked God to fix your life but keep grabbing it back because you don't think He is doing it fast enough? Just become aware of your thoughts and expectations regarding the one who loves you. Trust Him!

Remember to keep up with your separate prayer log journal. What prayers of yours for others have been answered? Note them in the log.

NOTES

Section Two
Love

Chapter Eight
Love of Self

In the last chapter, you transitioned and moved beyond the past, just like the twenty-third Psalm verse 4a says "**yea, though I walk through the shadow of death**"(KJV). Notice it was the through that you moved past. In this chapter, you may be charting new territory. This new territory is called *Love of Self*. I am going to have you rediscover many "self" words. You are going to analyze them for their positive and negative natures as you begin your *Love of Self*.

I want you to recall in Chapter Two, "Hurt Over Time", I likened the work you were doing to plastic surgery. The plastic surgery has healed; the bruising and trauma have gone from the areas. There is no visible (emotional) scar. The old scars are gone. Been removed. It is as if they were never there. So you can now forget about them.

Now, also recall in Chapter Three, "Healing Takes Time," you worked on the mortar of your self-esteem building blocks. Many of those blocks are going to be addressed again in this chapter in a more traditional way, using the self-words that are related to them. Love of self is called self-esteem and sometimes measured by self-worth. All of the building blocks (love, patience, positive awareness, centeredness, belief, tenderness, and self-talk) and the mortar created the self-esteem. Also, in Chapter Three I warned you that not enough love was as dangerous as too much love of self. In this chapter, I will cover the subject in much more depth.

I want you to notice the scale or balance below. Think of too much love on the low side because it is too heavy, and not enough love on the high side due to it being light. What you are going to be working for is a balance between the two dishes. You want them to be level and even-balanced.

Some self-words associated with too much love of self are self-absorbed, selfish, self-centeredness, self-indulgent, and self-righteous. Some self-words associated with not enough love of self are self-conscious, self-doubt, self-deprecation, self-pity and self-loathing.

While using one of your self-esteem building blocks mentioned in chapter three, Positive Awareness, I want you to become self-aware. Some self-words associated with a balanced or positive self-awareness are self-disciplined, self-directed, self-motivated, self-nurturing, self-improvement, self-discovery, and self-confident.

SELF-DISCIPLINED   **SELF-MOTIVATED**
SELF-CONFIDENT   **SELF-DIRECTED**
SELF-NURTURING   **SELF-DISCOVERY**

POSITIVE SELF-AWARENESS

Take a look at these self-words and analyze their part in your love of self. Remember you are developing, strengthening, and maintaining a positive self-esteem and a positive awareness of your self-worth. I will review the meaning of these words and place them on the scale for you. Later in the journal exercises, you will complete a similar task with more self-words.

Definitions and Placement of Self-Words on Scale

Too much love of self

Self-absorbed - preoccupied with one's thoughts, interests, etc.
Selfish - devoted to or caring only for oneself; concerned primarily with one's own interests, benefits, welfare, etc., regardless of others.
Self-centered - concerned solely or chiefly with one's own interests, welfare, etc.; engrossed in self; selfish; egotistical.
Self-indulgent - indulging one's own desires, passions, whims, etc., especially without restraint.
Self-righteous - confident of one's own righteousness, especially when smugly moralistic and intolerant of the opinions and behavior of others.

Balanced

Self-disciplined - discipline and training of oneself, usually for improvement
Self-directed - Directed or guided by oneself, especially as an independent agent
Self-motivated - initiative to undertake or continue a task or activity without another's prodding or supervision
Self-nurturing - To maintain one's own health and well-being
Self-improvement - improvement of one's mind, character, etc., through one's own efforts
Self-discovery - The act or process of achieving understanding or knowledge of oneself
Self-confident - realistic confidence in one's own judgment, ability, and power

Not enough love of self

Self-conscious - excessively aware of being observed by others and excessively conscious of one's appearance or manner
Self-doubt - lack of confidence in the reliability of one's own motives, personality, and thought
Self-deprecation - belittling or undervaluing oneself; excessively modest
Self-pity - pity for oneself, especially a self-indulgent attitude concerning one's own difficulties, and hardships
Self-loathing - extreme dislike of oneself, or being angry at oneself
All definitions from Webster's dictionary.

NOT ENOUGH	TOO MUCH
SELF-PITY	**SELFISH**
SELF-DOUBT	**SELF-CENTERED**
SELF-LOATHING	**SELF-RIGHTEOUS**
SELF-CONSCIOUS	**SELF-INDULGENCE**
SELF-DEPRESSION	**SELF-ABSORBED**

LOVE OF SELF

Now, even though I have defined these words and placed them on the scale, it is important also to realize that sometimes the self-words may actually be observed, but deep on a person's inside the opposite feeling is taking place. For instance, self-centered is displayed with egotistical behavior and selfishness is displayed by exhibiting behaviors of greediness and lack of concern for others. Yet these traits do not necessarily mean someone values themselves. They may actually feel inferior, imperfect, inadequate, unlovable, unworthy, or unintelligent. One uses traits of selfishness to camouflage the above listed feelings. Likewise, self-pity can also be just showing too much love of self and actually be an act of self-indulgence. These days, the label for this is "drama queen." Whereas, true self-esteem, the value of self, is demonstrated by patience with self, value of feelings, self examining and evaluating the reasons for feelings. A person with adequate self-esteem knows their strengths and weaknesses, uses their strengths and minimizes their weaknesses, and accepts others more easily. It is in the excessive display of some of these self-words that you get out of balance.

Become aware of your love of self. Analyze your traits and behaviors and determine whether you need to correct your individual balance. An example of a similar task is demonstrated at your eye doctor's office. Your eye doctor checks your eyesight. The doctor checks for farsightedness and nearsightedness. Then, if either is deficient to a large degree, the eye doctor will try different lenses and test to find the one you say corrects the vision problem. That is what I am asking you to do. You analyze the self-words and find out if your "self" vision is in need of a lens adjustment. Do you need to make a lens adjustment to your farsightedness so you don't stumble and hurt yourself? Or is it your nearsightedness that needs correcting so you can read the signs of caution accurately in life?

You ultimately are looking for balance, a true and accurate assessment of your abilities and attributes. By finding this balanced and accurate level of self-esteem, you achieve a healthy love of self. When you love yourself with corrected vision, then you can love others in the same way. It starts with you and love of self.

An extension of love of self is love of your children. Children are an extension of you. Remember, before taking off on a flight, the attendant goes through the safety instructions. One of the instructions is for you (the parent or adult) to secure your oxygen mask first before assisting your child with putting on their mask. The same is true with love of self. Love you then love them. The reason the attendant has to tell adults this is because we usually do it backwards. The norm is the children always come first and the parent comes last. Of course, the placement of the oxygen mask happens close to simultaneously, but you come first, assisting them right behind you. It is important to understand that you love your *self* so that you have love to give to them. Also, you are loving your *self* so that they learn to love their *self* from you. Now, just like on the plane, you come first, love of self, then simultaneously love of child.

There are age restrictions to these instructions. The child who is over 18 years of age is considered an adult, and that time response for love of child is different than for young children. If you have young children still in K-12 school, you can best love them by loving yourself first. The way you love yourself teaches them about life and loving themselves, as well as loving others. Mothers are known for sacrificing themselves for their children. There is a difference between sacrificing and nurturing. Nurturing is good for children. Sacrificing yourself is not ... of course, unless the truck is barreling down the road and you are trying to push them out of the street and don't have time to move out of the way yourself even though you thought you would. In most cases, this scenario seldom happens.

By nurturing yourself (meeting your needs), you best nurture your children and their needs. Fix food for everyone and sit down and eat together. Ask about your child's day and then briefly tell them about yours. Do house chores together. Everyone changes his or her own sheets. Everyone helps fold laundry. Everyone has (home or school) work time. Everyone has playtime. Everyone gets bath time and bedtime. Everyone means you as well as the children. You aren't and don't love yourself by doing it all while they play.

Crying on your children's shoulders about their dad (your ex) doesn't show love and respect for yourself or your children. Everyone needs down time. Share it with other adults, and if you have no other adult with which to share, then talk and cry with yourself in your own room behind closed doors. Have a 10 minute "Pity Party" and then move on to thinking about what you are going to do to make you feel good ... feel good about you. Love YOU! Love of Self.

Make a list of things you would love to do or get for yourself (under $20). Then list when you will, and check it off after the task is completed. It might mean you take yourself out on a date to get an ice cream cone all by yourself and relish licking every bit in peace and quiet. You be creative and think of some small pleasures. If you aren't checking anything off, you are not trying to love you. By loving you, you will find that you will feel good, will start looking good, and will be laughing more. Therefore, your children will reap the benefits. They will feel loved. Because when you say, "Sweetie, Mommy loves you," they will see it in your face.

Now, back to those adult children of yours (over age 18). They may be in college, or for some reason still living with you. They are old enough to take care of themselves and it is time you start teaching them how if you haven't yet. It is not good to enable them by doing everything for them because you're afraid if you don't, they will stop loving you, too. If they love you, they will love you even when they have to do work to take care of themselves. They may be a little shocked at the change, but it had to come sometime. You can spend time with them while they are completing their chores, since you may have to instruct (not do) on how to use the washing machine, cut the grass, rake the leaves and even make a bed. You can get updated on their lives while they work, because you know when the task is done, they will split and not be seen. It is time to let them go. Buy them a copy of this book to read; some of the exercises could do them good, and then release them in Love.

You have been through separation/divorce and never thought that it would happen to you when you set out on the marriage road. But it did. However, through it all you have found stamina, willpower, energy, and courage to go on. It is through facing adversity that you grow emotionally and spiritually. Give yourself recognition for the stamina, will power, energy, and courage that you have displayed. It wasn't easy, but you did it. Next, complete the journal and prayer journal exercises. And don't forget to work on your list of small pleasures; it might actually bring a smile to your face. Remember, you are past **Time**. It is now time to feel **Love** ... **Love of Self**.

NOTES

Chapter Eight – Love of Self
RESOURCES

Movies (dvd,tv,etc.)

Shop Girl (2005)

Songs

Books/Articles/Groups/Other Resources
(and articles on the internet)

Ellis, A. and Bernard, M. (Eds.) (1985). *Applications of Rational Emotive Therapy*, New York: Plenum Publishing Co.

Psychology Today on the Web

>Your Trump Card: Self-Love By:Hara Estroff Marano
>www.psychologytoday.com/articles/pto-20021203-000002.html

>The Lion Tamer - Article about Steven Stosny By:Cecilia Capuzzi Simon
>www.psychologytoday.com/articles/index.php?term=pto-20050615-000003&page=1

Psychiatrists, Psychotherapists, and Psychologists

Albert Ellis

Resources I found related to this chapter?

_____

_____

NOTES

Case Study #8

Donna was divorced, and had been now for 9 years. She had had two serious relationships which had lasted three years each before she ended them, realizing she was not "in Love" with them enough to get married again. She did not want to settle for a marriage relationship that was not all that she wanted: one filled with romance, passion, and deep, abiding friendship. I guess you could say she was looking for her soul mate.

What she did find was that the relationships were necessary for her continued development. With the first relationship, she learned she was worthy of love. She learned to treat herself good. She learned to do nice things for herself. She also learned she did not have to depend on someone else to do that for her, but that she could provide that love and acceptance herself.

The second relationship taught her to be a child again. Somehow she had put away childish things the day she got married, and met all responsibility seriously. She had forgotten how to play and be silly and laugh. She began learning how to even laugh at herself. She also learned even though she laughed at herself, she was not condemning herself just because she saw faults or mistakes.

An example of her confidence is seen in the telling of an event, which took place in 1999. It was New Year's Eve. She had received an invitation to go to New York City to celebrate the turning of the century. She had been listening to all the hype for months about Y2K. She decided to turn down the invite and stay at home. That was a difficult decision since she had an opportunity to go there when she was 18, but her parents prohibited it. Now, she was being asked again to go, and she was prohibiting it for safety reasons. But this did not mean she did not have a great time. She planned her own personal party. She took a bubble bath in the afternoon. She got really dressed up and went out to the video store. She picked up two movies she had been dying to see. She then stopped at the grocery store and bought a filet mignon steak and some fresh vegetables. She stopped off and picked up some pinot noir to accompany the fine dinner she was planning.

Her plans included watching one movie, having dinner, and then watching the second movie. Next, she would check the news for some of the locations which would be turning 2000 first, to see if all was well. Then, she was going to bed with her alarm set for 11:45 p.m. so that she could get up to watch the ball drop in New York and the fireworks on the east coast. Much to her pleasure, at the end of the second movie there were two music videos. The songs were in the

Top 40. She got up to dance to them both, then fell into her chair laughing and truly enjoying herself. She was able to watch fireworks televised from Sydney, Australia and Paris, France.

Some may think, "how could any of that give pleasure?" For Donna, it brought pleasure because she had planned it herself and it was everything that she enjoyed doing with the one person who loved her the most ... Her self!

Chapter Eight – Love of Self
Journal

In this chapter's journal exercises, I am asking you to take a look at some other self-words. You will look up the meanings and place them on the scales. Then you will evaluate where you stand on the practice of the word(s) in your life.

Exercise 1

Write out the definitions to the following self-words below.

Self-sufficient -
_____
_____

Self-realization -
_____
_____

Self-analysis -
_____
_____

Self-critical -
_____
_____

Self-aggrandizement -
_____
_____

Self-abasement -
_____
_____

Self-assurance -
_____
_____

Self-reproaching -
_____
_____

Self-enrichment -
_____
_____

Self-reliant -
_____
_____

Self-despair -
_____
_____

Self-educated -
_____
_____

Self-justification -
_____
_____

Self-deception -
_____
_____

Self-sacrifice -
_____
_____

     Now, go back and place a notation next to each word indicating its placement on the "self" scale. TM for a word showing too much love of self, B for a balanced amount of self love, and NE for a word that indicates not enough love of self. (Hint: There are an uneven number in each category)

Exercise 2
List 15 more self-words that you have found while looking up the ones above. Write out each definition and place a notation to indicate its placement on the scale.

Self-_____
_____
_____

Self-_____
_____
_____

Self-_____
_____
_____

Self-_____
_____
_____

Self-_____
_____
_____

Self-_____
_____
_____

Self-_____
_____
_____

Self-_____
_____
_____

Self-_____
_____
_____

Self-_____
_____
_____

Self-_____

_____
_____

Self-_____

_____
_____

Self-_____

_____
_____

Self-_____

_____
_____

Self-_____

_____
_____

Exercise 3

On the picture of the scale on the next page, write in the self-words that you feel you need to work on. Then, use positive awareness over the next month as you go through your normal routines to note when you have displayed the behavior. Remember you are not going to admonish yourself when you realize you have displayed the behavior. You only need to be aware of it.

Eventually, if you intend for the behavior to change, your sub-conscious mind will take care of it for you. That is just a factor of NLP that I was introducing you to before. You tell your conscious mind you want to do something and your sub-conscious mind will take care of it for you. You just have to be aware of when that something is occurring. It sounds too simple, but it is that easy. You usually need to take some time doing quiet meditative work on the subject for the process to be most effective, but it does produce results. If you haven't yet read up on NLP, for now just use your knowledge of positive awareness to note your behaviors. Then, tell yourself you will research this technique in the near future.

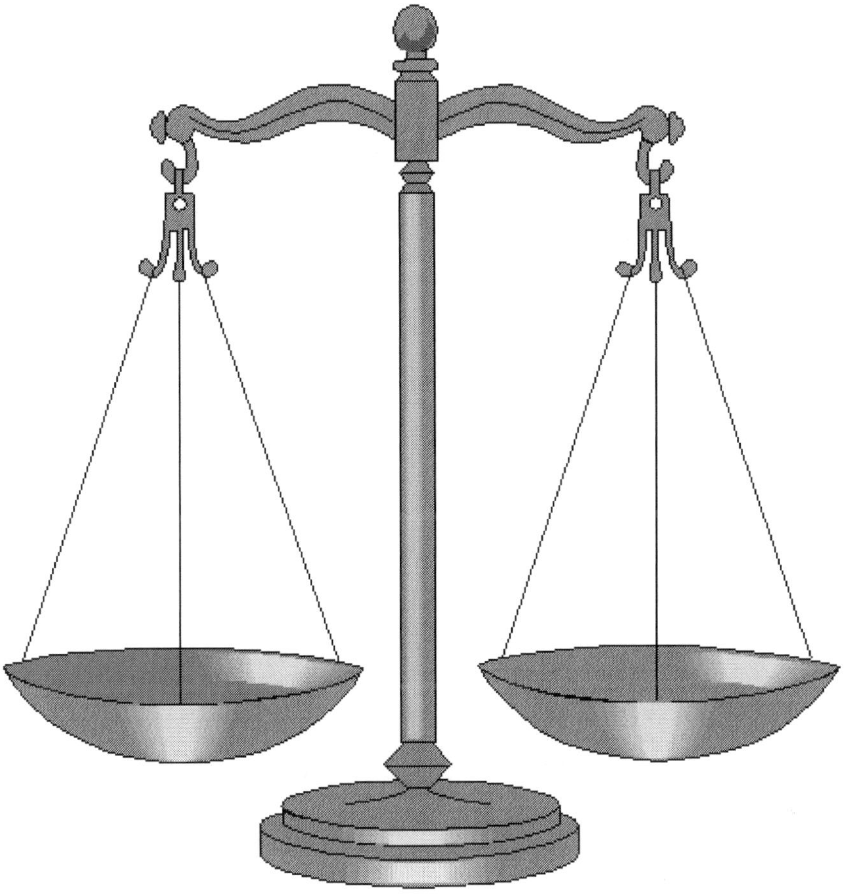

NOTES

Chapter Eight – Love of Self
Prayer Journal

Begin your time by praying and thanking God. Ask God to see yourself as He sees you. Be still and listen to Him. Close your prayer in thanks and praise.

You have probably heard people say, "God doesn't make Junk." Sometimes, you look at yourself so critically that you think that you are so flawed that God couldn't possible love you. This is not true. Being God, He knew that man was not going to be perfect, yet He created him anyway. He knew that man would choose wrongly, but He gave him free will anyway. God is an awesome parent of man. He sees us just as we are and loves us anyway. He loved us before He made us. He loves us even though our promises are broken. He loves justly. He does not enable us. He teaches us responsibility and humility. Let Him teach you to have pride, but not be prideful. Remember, you are the child of God. He loves you because you are worth something and He made you that way. It is not boastful to see your worth through God's eyes.

Scripture Reading

How is this done? Look at David's life. He was said in scripture to have a whole heart for God. Yet, he was not perfect.

Read 1 Samuel 17:34.

How did David accurately evaluate himself and his abilities to the king when he was a boy?

_____
_____
_____
_____

Read 2 Samuel 12.

Later in David's life, how did he see himself? How did God help him?

_____
_____
_____
_____

Read 1 Kings 15:3-5.

What does it say about David?

_____
_____
_____
_____

Remember, that how you act and react is <u>your</u> choice. You can decide to be beautiful or ugly as a witch or toad.

Choose to be beautiful because you are. God made you whole. He gave you everything you need in this life. Choose to realize it, to appreciate it, and to value it. Your Heavenly Father does and He shows it with His love. Now, you show it with your love of self. It is your choice. You are in charge. Choose to love again. But start with you!

Section Two
Love

Chapter Nine
Love of Friends

In this chapter, I want you to take a look at your *Love of Friends*. Love is a two-way street. You give and you get love and you get love and you give love. This is true in friendships. Sometimes, you get love from one friendship and give it in another friendship. Either way love can not be held onto and stored away; it must be shared in order to reap any benefits that it has to offer. A friend of mine once said that the giver of love is the one that reaps the benefits, not the receiver. The receiver may receive gifts, but does not experience the feeling in the heart that the giver has. Only if the receiver feels love for a person and gives love back does the receiver benefit and actually become the giver instead. It was an odd statement, but the more I thought about it, I realized how true it was. You want to be loved, but the feelings really come when you give love and it is accepted. *Love of Friends* is a good place to begin when looking at love given and received outside your *self* and your children.

There are many types of friends. There are true friends from childhood and from adulthood. There are true friends you found in married years and those found in divorce years. There will be friends found in moving-on years. I want you to take a closer look at each of these. Your true friends from childhood know you. They know all about you, yet they still want to be with you, and you with them. Then there are the true friends you developed in adulthood while you were married. They stayed your friend and supported you during your divorce. During the divorcing years, others like you, who understand the pains of divorce, who have survived or are learning how to survive, have become your friends. Their understanding and support have meant a lot to you. Soon, you will develop your moving-on years friends. They will be made up of survivors. They are the strong supportive ones who, like you, have "passed through the valley of death and fear no evil." You will have a varied cadre of friends that you have met and developed throughout your life, through your ups and your downs. Some go so far as to say the devil gives us our families and God gives us our friends. There are some who realize they have spent their whole life developing friends only to find out that they were as messed up as their family. Whereas for others, members of your family have been your closest supportive friends, and still some others of you may have found they were your worst enemies on this battlefield of divorce. The point I am making is to take a look at your true friends, whomever they may be, and however and whenever you acquired them.

True friends are rare. Usually, you will find that the two-way street definitely operates within the friendship. You give as much love as you receive from this one person. It seems you are both givers and not both receivers. There isn't anything you or your friend wouldn't do for the other. You may have found this with your childhood friends. It may be still true. It may be that you share history with them and that is comforting to both of you. In other cases, some of your history isn't shared anymore and it makes it difficult to have the same closeness as a newer true friend. Sometimes, true friends exist for a short time as if God knew you needed them and they needed you. That is okay. True friends don't always mean forever. God provides what you need as you need it.

Now, I want you to look at these true friends and think about why you love them? What do you get out of it? You do get something out of it or you wouldn't or won't need or want them. How do they make you feel? Do they make you feel... wanted, loved, supported, understood, needed, uplifted, alive, centered, peaceful, grounded, important, needed, heard, valued, necessary, cared for, accepted? Now, I want you to look at what they get from you. Identify why they want you for a friend. You supply them with feelings just as you have had feelings because of their friendship. You serve a purpose. The street is a two-way street. Love flows in and it flows out. It is good to analyze and realize that you have been giving love as you have been receiving love over the course of time that marks your separation and divorce.

    The next group of friends is made because of your social settings. The social settings may be found at church; on committees, clubs and organizations; and/or in neighborhoods. These friends are persons you have connected with due to shared activities or locations. Some of these friends may have become true friends, but usually not. This group of friends gives you a sense of belonging. You enjoy sharing the activity with them. At church you share your faith, and are encouraged spiritually. There may be a women's or men's group that get together for social events and at other times they gather to do service activities. Social groups and civic organizations can also provide you a place to serve and help others. Activity and sports groups are made up of people with whom to enjoy cards, jogging, roller blading, bowling, dancing, etc. Neighborhoods give you neighbors that share your concerns related to the area in which you live. This group of friends serves its purpose in your life as well. The type of love given in these groups is not on a deep level like the love you and a true friend share, yet it is just as necessary in providing you with a sense of belonging and providing you a place to express yourself with like-minded persons.

    The next group of friends may be social at times, but usually is not. It is made up of your work mates. These are people you didn't really select, but those you do come in contact with and who influence your quality of life and you influence theirs. They may have known about your divorce first or it may have been the last group to know. To love, you must trust and feel vulnerable – love at work is usually not this type of love, it is not a deep love. The work, place may provide a feeling of belonging like the social groups. If your workplace feels like a place you can belong, work is easier to perform and the day may be tough, but it seems to fly by quicker. The boss, as well as the workers, are responsible for this feeling of belonging. Each worker has to be valued and appreciated and acknowledged. Good businesses have recognized this and have tried promoting it. There are activities that some employers have used to improve their customer service. These activities start with the employees. They are team building activities. Through these activities, trust and mutual appreciation are developed. The philosophy is, that if the team of workers work together with trust and acceptance, the workers will coordinate their efforts to improve the customer service that is being provided. If good customer service is given, the business will grow and thrive. Sometimes, these activities work, and other times it is difficult to create the right environment. So, even though trust and acceptance are demonstrated, if love is given, it is limited. There is so much more to love than that. Yet, you are giving and receiving limited love at work if there is this trust and acceptance demonstrated there. This group of friends (work mates) serves its purpose in your life as well. The type of love given is just as necessary in providing you with a sense of belonging and providing you a place to demonstrate your abilities with persons that are also trained to achieve work related goals. You have been trained to understand and to demonstrate the related tasks. Each of your co-workers may have different tasks, but together you achieve the goals. You belong to a workforce.

  Your friends, whether they be close friends or be made up of varying acquaintance levels, provide you with a chance to love, to be loved, and to belong. As you analyze the love you give and get from your friends, you will understand more fully their importance to you. Use the journal and prayer journal in this chapter to analyze your Love of Friends before moving on to the next chapter.

Chapter Nine – Love of Friends
RESOURCES

Movies (dvd,tv,etc.)

Dinner with Friends (2001)

Songs

Books/Articles/Groups/Other Resources
　　(and articles on the internet)

Fowler, Lynda K. (1998), *Friendships in Adulthood SS-141-98*, Ohio State University Extension. http://ohioline.osu.edu/ss-fact/0141.html

Yokoyama, John and Michelli, Joseph Ph.D. (2004). *When Fish Fly: Lessons for Creating A Vital And Energized Workplace From The World Famous Pike Place Fish Market*, New York: Hyperion
ISBN: 1-4013-0061-8

Psychiatrists, Psychotherapists, and Psychologists

Robert Glaser

Resources I found related to this chapter?
_____
_____
_____
_____

NOTES

Case Study #9

Christina was 35 years old and divorced from her husband. She had a daughter. Christina was transferred by her company to a new location and lived in a different state from her ex-husband. The daughter went to visit her father for two weeks in the summer. Christina was told about a prayer group that met to pray before work once a week. She began attending and met another woman, Kathy, who worked in her building. Eventually, they talked and became better acquainted. They found they had a lot in common beside their obvious belief in God. One other thing they had in common was that they were recently divorced and looking for new friends.

Both Christina and Kathy had children near the same age. They began to visit at each other's homes and would meet to shop at the mall on the weekend. Neither could afford a babysitter, but the children did not get in the way of them all spending time together. At Christmas time, they found free concerts and activities in their area to attend. For Christina and Kathy, it was the first Christmas since their divorce and when the Christmas holidays came, neither of them would be having the children because the children were going to the ex-husbands' houses. They both knew it was going to be a tough time but due to their new friendship of several months it made it much more enduring. They helped each other decorate their homes and bought gifts for each other for Christmas day. It was the first time either of them could remember that they slept in on Christmas morning. They had planned to meet up and go to a movie Christmas afternoon and then go over to Kathy's house for dinner.

As time passed, the children grew up and went off to college and got married. Christina and Kathy ended up meeting someone after dating over the years, and each got married again. Somehow, the two couples didn't work like the two gals had. They both relocated after retirement and now only communicate through Christmas cards. Their friendship had served a purpose through their single parent years, and now they had moved on and made new close friends with their husbands. They were both thankful to God for supplying a friendship when they needed it most.

Even though life changes, it is good to accept that friendships do also. Childhood friends sometimes don't become adult friends and yet, adult friends can never take the place of talking over "the good ole days" with your best buddy from grade and high school. Life takes it turns and we change with it on the inside as well as out.

NOTES

Chapter Nine – Love of Friends
Journal

In this chapter's journal exercises, be thoughtful and truthful as you answer the questions.

There is an internet circulated document that tells about friendship; you may have seen it. It tells how we each have friends that fit into three categories: ones for reasons, ones for seasons and ones for a lifetime. What is important is for you to be able to see the purpose and importance of friendship.

I want you to think about your friends.

1. Who are your childhood-acquired friends?

2. Who are your adult-acquired friends?

3. At what stage(s) in life did you acquire the adult friends?

4. What friends have you acquired since the separation?

5. Go back and list beside each name listed above the commonality that caused you to become friends.

6. Categorize your lifetime of friends into three groups:

For A Season	For A Reason	For A Lifetime
_____	_____	_____
_____	_____	_____
_____	_____	_____
_____	_____	_____
_____		

7. What have you learned or how have you benefited from their friendships?

_____
_____
_____
_____
_____
_____
_____
_____

8. How did they benefit by having you as a friend?

_____
_____
_____
_____
_____
_____
_____
_____

Chapter Nine – Love of Friends
Prayer Journal

Remember to open your prayer journal time with prayer and thanksgiving. Thank God for the many friendships you have had throughout your lifetime. Pray for each of your old friends as well as new friends one by one.

Read the story of David and Jonathan's friendship in 1 Samuel 18-20, 1 Samuel 23:15-18, 2 Samuel 1, and 2 Samuel 9.

1. What caused them to become friends?

2. What did David get from his friendship with Jonathan?

3. What did Jonathan get from his friendship with David?

4. How long did their friendship last?

5. Can you find any other friendships listed in the Bible? Name two and analyze the purpose of those friendships. What did each friend get out of being a friend?

6. Who is a friend with whom you can share your faith? How do you do that?

Section Two
Love

Chapter Ten
Love of Dating

In this chapter, I want you to take a look at your *Love Of Dating*. I want you to analyze why you want to date, what you expect to get out of dating, how to begin to date again, and what you will find when searching for a dating relationship again. I am going to give you advice and cautions. You may love excitement, entertainment, and to experience something new and different, but your *Love Of Dating* isn't LOVE. Don't be afraid to set some parameters before you begin dating again. Know what you want and get what you want.

If you are a person who just got out of an abusive relationship alive, you may consider yourself lucky. A broken heart is nothing to suffer compared to the emotional scars and physical injuries that can be caused by physical abuse. You don't ever think you will be able to trust anyone enough to get involved again. Some women find themselves fooled again by the con artists who convince her that they are to be trusted, loved and respected. Some women find themselves pregnant because they become emotionally attached. They believe the convincing act and believe they are being really loved this time. How does she believe that? Well, it is easy. They have all their lives just wanted to be protected and loved. Because they are so vulnerable, they can't see the obvious. If you are recovering from an abusive relationship, be sure to take the time to love your *self* before loving someone else. Don't tie yourself down. Learn to be free and independent. Through your independence, you will gain all the skills that you will need to enter into a relationship with your eyes wide open. With your eyes wide open, you will be able to catch all the warning signs that something is not all right here. As they say, "If it is too good to be true, then it is!"

Look for support groups to assist you and avail yourself to every self-help aide you can get your hands on. Watch pop psychologists who clearly show persons with similar issues and give very practical advice. But a little word of advice here, don't become a TV psychologist junkie viewing everyone else's problems and forgetting to focus on you. You must keep working on your *self*... building your *self* up and growing.

Some other information which may be good for you to look into, is assertiveness training. It could be beneficial for you. You could learn to assert yourself and protect your rights way before events get to a stage of being threatening. This is also important before you get back into a relationship of dependency again. Another topic to research and study is co-dependency. Evaluate if you have been operating under a co-dependency model most of your life. These are all good topics even if you do not exactly fall into the perfect description of those categories. Just be careful and proceed with great caution when heading back into the dating scene. Decide what signs will assure you that the person you are going to date has truly earned your trust, especially before giving away your heart. See things clearly without emotional attachments.

Just like the warning that was given to the abused, it is important to learn how to judge the person who is going to be the next dating relationship. You don't want to be a bum magnet. No, I am not saying, to go around judging everyone. I am saying know what you are looking for. What traits are going to be absolutely necessary before you are going to give your heart again? What traits need to be visible before you even date once?

Yes, I really want you to make a list of what you are looking for. Dream of the perfect mate and list what that is. I have been told that counterfeit experts study the real money very carefully. They never study the counterfeit bills. They want to know the real thing so well that when they see the counterfeit bill it is very obvious to them. So, when you make your list of perfection (as you value it to be) you will know when something is amiss ... not what you want. Also, like the abused, you will be able to recognize when someone is displaying controlling behaviors indicating warning signs in bright neon lights flashing on and off saying, "Quick! Run Now! Run, don't walk to the closest EXIT."

Be careful when trying to feel loved again that you don't draw in the types that you don't really want. First off, it can be dangerous, and second, it is not fair to reject others after doing such a beautiful and convincing sell job just so you can feel good about yourself and say, "Look, I'm desirable." Others have feelings too.

So, how do you gather information without getting your heart involved? First, you need to know what you like. What activities do you like? Go do them by yourself. Yes, I said go do them by yourself. Learn to do things alone. Learn to be by yourself. Learn to live with quiet, no radios and televisions going from sunup to sundown (or even on all night). Some of you may be actually afraid of being with your *self*. It is difficult to be able to do any life changing work if you do not take any quiet time to accomplish it. Learn to not need others to provide activity for you, but provide it for yourself.

If you like going out to dinner and haven't gone since last you remember, then select the restaurant that you would like to go to and plan to treat yourself to a dinner date. I suggest that you go at the beginning of the dinner hour and not take a book. Take your *self* only. Try a test, see if you can have an appetizer, dinner, and dessert, and do so as slowly as possible. Even use the restroom before dinner is served or right after you order the dessert to help pace yourself. I tried this once and was so proud of myself because I ended up taking almost two hours. I usually can't eat that much, so I ordered the appetizer and then another appetizer (that seemed large for one) as the entrée with a side salad. I also ordered from the beginning the best chocolate dessert that they had with a cappuccino. I gave the waiter the instructions to not place the dinner portion of my order until he saw that I had finished my glass of water. My goal was to take at least an hour and to pace myself slowly as if I was on a date with someone and was having dinner conversation. That evening there were two women, who were seated right after me, who had their dinners and left as I was being served my dessert. I enjoyed my *self* so much that I decided to take my *self* out to dinner once each month.

The next month, when I went out to dinner, I saw another woman by herself. After my appetizer, I went over and asked if she would like me to join her, but only if she was feeling awkward or too alone. She said she would like the company. We talked and got acquainted. She was in my town on business, which was probably a good thing, so that I did not develop a lasting friendship. I might have forgotten my goal of enjoying my company. But I did learn how to gather information in conversation without it seeming like interrogation, and to do so without interest in making someone else think I was cute and adorable.

As I gathered information about my dinner company, you too will need to gather information about your perspective dates the same way. Know what you are getting into. Have they been married? How long did the marriage last? Did they have children? What are the ages of the children? How actively involved are they in their lives? What are their responsibilities in rearing the children? Where do they live? A friend of mine even went so far as to have a police friend of hers tell her if the new person she was interested in dating had ever been arrested. Even though that would be useful information, most of us can't get that information. Some persons would even gather information about the date's financial history. It does not mean necessarily that you are a gold digger if you would be interested in this type of information. If you don't have any debt, you will not want to be linked with a debtor. But if you are steeped in debt, remember it is not their responsibility to pay for yours either. Money is an important issue. Many marital fights involve the issue of money and spending money. It is good to also know one's financial perspectives on life before the heart is involved. So ,somewhere early in dating you may want to broach the subject before you decide to make it a permanent dating and marriage relationship.

    Other information you will want to gather, involves personality traits. Some people are laid back, others are anxious. Some people are morning-people. Others are night owls. Some are planners; others are spontaneous. Some are those that cling, they want to be together all the time; others flee, they love being independent and together for social occasions only. You have heard the old adage "Opposites Attract," and of course they do. It complements our personalities. They are everything we are not and might wish to be. The problem is that it is hard to live in a constant state of tug-of-war. You need compatibility. There are a number of personality and compatibility tests out there. Sometimes the tests are used as career compatibility tools. If you have ever taken one and know where to get one for your dating partner to take, it could be quite revealing. Myers/Briggs is a well-known type indicator test. Usually, you will need a professional trained in the interpretation of the test to administer it as well. You may find some on the Internet, but I don't know how reliable they are. Those that have 100+ questions are more accurate.

    Compatibility is something that your internal indicators can tell you. After each date, keep a separate notebook and fill it with information that you gathered. Notations on likes and dislikes, traits, philosophies regarding different topics such as religion, money, rearing of children, marriage roles, as well as intellectual and physical interests and activities. As you make your notations, you may also note your own. Maybe you have never evaluated yourself in this way before and it may bring new incites to the real you. Gather your information and let your mind, as well as your heart, make decisions when it comes to love in dating.

You may have friends who have or will be able to set you up with blind dates with single persons that they know and you have never met. At least, you have one recommendation coming from the mutual friend, which you trust. You may have already exhausted their list of friends to date or you don't have any friends offering to play matchmaker. In that case, you may be saying, "Where do I find a date?" Especially if you dated your ex in high school and were married 20+ years, you may not have any idea. Some of the frequently used places are bars, activity groups, church, work, singles groups, and the Internet. I will cover each of these places, evaluating them negatively and/or positively in the next few paragraphs.

Bars are often used to meet people because mostly singles frequent a bar at night. On the weekends, there is music and dancing to attract singles. Some problems with bars are 1) they are usually filled with smoke, 2) they are filled with people drinking and a favorite hangout for alcoholics, 3) they have a higher ratio of users and losers. Most of these you don't want in your home forever and ever. If you don't fit into the 4 categories, the chances are your future date is not there because he doesn't either. But go and find out for yourself. There may be a slight chance that your new partner is there for the first time just like you, but more than likely not. Just be warned.

Activity groups are centered on various physical activities such as skiing, bowling, amateur astronomy, roller blading, and bicycling. All types of persons belong to activity groups, not just singles. It gives you a chance to get out and do something with people and make new friends. It also builds a new support group of friends and gives you something new to talk about and not spend all your time rehashing the past.

Church is also a good place to meet persons with your spiritual interests. Churches sometimes have separated/divorced support groups. Your particular denomination may not have one, but another church near you just may have one to use for the purpose of Christian support and meeting like-situation persons. At your home church, you may find a men's or women's fellowship group, as well as a service-oriented group to help the unfortunate. These groups are beneficial for those being helped, but also for the helpers because it makes you more thankful for what you have been blessed with.

Work can provide more than just income. It sometimes gives the opportunity to meet new people in various settings. One thing is sure, you must be very careful dating workmates and/or clients. Some companies have policies forbidding dating. If a dating relationship doesn't work out with a workmate or client, it can get ugly in the work place. So, be cautious in looking for love in the wrong places.

Singles groups, whether church oriented or not, do exist. A word of precaution on any singles group, they are sometimes known as "meat markets." Of course, that doesn't mean they all are. Some persons who attend them for years on end use the group for finding new, easy prey. The newbie (new divorcee) is vulnerable, gullible, and naive. So go into the lion's den prepared and aware.

Some think that all blind dates are the same, that being set up by your friend doesn't differ from having a blind date with a date, from a personal ad or the Internet. If you are going to try this avenue of finding a date be sure to set certain parameters before you start. The persons you will meet will not come with recommendations like the blind dates that your friends set for you. Also, these possible dates are not known by anyone you know, unlike the groups of new people you are meeting that I have mentioned before. In those other groups, at least the fellow members know each other. So think through what you are looking for in a dating partner and accurately and truly list traits and likes of yours. Take a first warning: Some People Lie. They pretend to be single when they are really married. They pretend to be old when they are underage. They pretend to be young when they are old. They even pretend to be ... anything that will attract someone. So there are users and losers there, also, but there are in the drug, alcohol, and smoke free environment of your computer room. I belonged to and researched several single websites. One evening, I came home on a Friday night after a hard week. I fixed myself a little plate of food and sat down at the computer. I read profiles, looked at pictures, and at 9 p.m. I shut down the computer and went to bed. It was much more pleasant than the bar scene. I measured people up to my standard and no one bothered me. It was comfortable in my own home and I got to go to bed at my usual time on a Friday night instead of just beginning to start the evening. If you are going to pursue the Internet scene, research different singles sites. Go to Google and search, basically interview, these providers. See what ones you trust. Some are free to women. I found a Christian site years ago. I liked it best because of the profile requirements and the essay questions. Every one had to be answered before you could communicate with anyone. I found it was easy to see the fakes from those that were sincere. Unfortunately, I found no one that lived in my area that I was interested in dating. The ones I liked lived in other states. I met some, but I realized I needed to see someone more often before I could have a strong feeling of trust. I also found that if we did get seriously involved, one of us would have to move if it resulted in marriage. Most persons will not pull up stakes and move to a new place they have never lived, a place where they don't know anyone except this one person they met on the Internet. During this time, I did meet a woman that did just that, she moved from the East Coast to the West Coast in the name of love. One year after marriage, she was divorcing again because of the big mistake she had made. She found him to not be anything like she thought him to be. He ended up being controlling and abusive. So, I pulled my geographical requirements in closer to home. I did develop Internet friends and persons to ask their opinion about certain situations. I developed some strong safety parameters. These are the ones I developed for me:

1. Meet in a safe, public area.

2. Never give directions to your home.

3. Never get into a stranger's car. You both drive to the meeting place. If you agree to meet at a mall, you can park in a safe location. Don't let the chivalrous walk you to your car at this point. You can, after meeting, shop slowly through the mall and make sure you are not being followed home. Don't give out your home phone number, until you feel safe (a person can get your address from your home number)

.4. Meet with them for an hour in a public food place like they have in malls. And at the end of the hour, decide whether to meet again. Notify them via the web, just like you set up the date to begin with. If there is a desire to go on, on both of your parts, you will continue to communicate through the computer. If not, someone will not answer back and rejection is much easier for both.

5. Remember people lie!

6. You decide when you should go out on dates in the more old-fashioned way, where the date comes to your home and picks you up and returns you home at the end of the date. This will take different lengths of time for different persons. Just be very sure before giving out your personal information related to your location through address, phone number and automobile description.

Many web sites ask you to check off a long list of your likes and dislikes. You can learn more in reading the profile than you can by dating a person for a month (4-6 dates). Just remember in deciding to date again, do so using your brain and not because you are desperate to be with the opposite sex again.

One of the things you are going to have to develop before dating is your communication skill. You don't want to give or receive mixed messages. Some of the reasons for your separation and/or divorce may be poor communication skills. It does not hurt to brush up on your communication skills. You do not want to be saying one thing and have your date get a different message. Several books have been written on the subject of communication between the sexes and also the miscommunication between the sexes. It is amazing what I learned about my communication through reading several of these books. I recommend you read books on the subject of marriage written by divorcees as well as persons that have been married to one person happily for many, many years. They both have much to offer when it comes to being successful in relationships. You will want to approach this issue of love in dating and **Love of Dating** with as much information and newly acquired skills as necessary in order to be successful, if life takes you back to a serious loving relationship again.

Now for my final warnings:

1. Take it easy. Go slow. Proceed with caution.

2. Don't run in before you look.

3. Be careful about those that prey on the rejected.

4. Excitement isn't love. Don't get confused.

5. Don't give it all! Save some of your heart (for Love of You, Love of Family, Love of Friends, and a possible future Love In Marriage.)

Be sure to use the journal exercises before entering the dating scene. It is best to be wise, think things through thoroughly, and be prepared for many situations and scenarios. Set your parameters. Determine what your authentic bill looks like so that you can recognize the counterfeit fakes. The exercises in this chapter's journal will help you think through all of this and your **Love of Dating**.

NOTES

Chapter Ten – Love of Dating
RESOURCES

Movies (dvd,tv,etc.)

Urban Cowboy (1980)

Songs

Lookin' for Love lyrics by Wanda Mallette, Patti Ryan and Bob Morrison

Books/Articles/Groups/Other Resources
(and articles on the internet)

Smith, Blaine (June 15, 2004). *Trust Your Judgement*, Nehemiah Notes. http://nehemiahministries.com

Myers-Briggs Type Indicator
http://www.personalitypathways.com/type_inventory.html

Google search engine on the Internet
www.Google.com

Parents Without Partners
http://www.parentswithoutpartners.org/

Gray, John (1992). *Men Are From Mars, Women Are From Venus*, New York: HarperCollins ISBN 0-06-057421-6

Gray, John (2000). *How To Get What You Want and Want What You Have*, New York: HarperCollins ISBN 0-06-093215-5

Gray, John (2003). *Mars and Venus On a Date*, New York: Vermilion (RAND) ISBN 0-09-188767-4

Psychiatrists, Psychotherapists, and Psychologists

John Gray

NOTES

Case Study #10

Debbie was 40 years old and separated from her husband. She attended a support group in her area. Once a year near Valentine's Day the members who were divorced put on a dinner for the members who were separated. It was a dress-up affair with tablecloths and flowers. This activity was meant to minister to the hurting separated persons, showing there was hope that "this too shall pass." At the dinner, a divorcee sat down beside her. She did not recognize him at first, but found out through conversation that they had been neighbors on the same street some 15 years before. She then recalled being in his home once. After the dinner he asked if she would like to go out to get more coffee. Debbie thought that there was no harm in it since she did meet him at church and vaguely knew him. They drove separately to a downtown area and walked around a park, talking and enjoying each other's company, and had some coffee. Then they parted.

He called her everyday after that. At the end of two weeks, she began sensing something was not quite right. One Saturday at the mall, he wrote a check and the clerk said his name was on the store's "not to accept" list. The next day, Debbie returned one of his calls only to find his phone had been disconnected. The next time he called explaining the disconnection, she told him that she wasn't really ready for dating anyway and she would see him at church on Sunday.

That ended up not working. He kept calling. She began to screen each call. He began writing letters that were typed and in business envelopes disguising whom they were from. He began saying in the letters "God told me you were meant for me." He even came to her house and left roses at her front door without knocking. She had an odd front porch that had steps that when stepped on would vibrate through the house usually announcing someone at the door before they knocked or rang the doorbell. She had been home, yet she had never heard anything. She really became worried.

She began to think of serious safety precautions. She already had a security system on the house. She bought timers for all her lamps. Her car was always in the garage and out of sight. Before it got dark, she would take her dinner upstairs and eat in her bedroom where she could not be seen through any window, and stayed there until morning. Two nights a week she attended classes at a university. She lived at the end of a dead end street and was concerned about the late hour that she arrived home after class. She decided if ever she saw a car at her house when she arrived home, she would turn around and drive directly to the police station.

All of these precautions did not stop him from writing or calling. He began calling her at work daily. The switchboard operator recognized his voice and would ask to take a message but he would not leave one. He next came to her workplace. One morning, she saw his car on the lot. She called her boss and asked for him not to be left unattended in the building for her own safety. Next, he met a student who was in one of Debbie's classes and enlisted her aid in luring Debbie to a bar under false pretense. Debbie didn't understand why the girl was befriending her and felt something was strange, so even though she accepted the invite, Debbie just went directly home. When the course ended, the fellow student told Debbie that it had been a setup to get Debbie there so he could talk with her. This type of stalking continued for over a year.

I write this as a warning. You never know who might be a stalker. This is not a fictional case study. Stalkers really do exist and they aren't only after or following the movie stars.

Chapter Ten – Love of Dating
Journal

In this chapter's journal exercises, I am asking you to think about what you really want. Be thoughtful and truthful as you answer the questions. Dream about the type of date you want, but be realistic about describing the real you.

1. Describe yourself to a blind person. Describe yourself in detail. Include all the details someone would need to know in order to pick you out in a crowd. Try to use one word descriptors.

2. Why do you want to date?

3. What do you expect to get out of dating?

4. What parameters will you set before you begin to date again?

5. What do you expect to find when searching for a date?

6. Testing your knowledge base

    a) What are some of the premises of assertiveness training?

    b) Identify a co-dependent person using the descriptors of co-dependency.

7. List several different types of singles and support groups in your area, List main emphasis and phone number. Consider your participation.

Name of support group   emphasis   phone number

8. What traits must someone display before you date them once?

9. What you are looking for in a dating partner?

10. What activities do you like?

11. List questions you will use to gather information on perspective dates.

12. Next to each of my final warnings, explain why that is a warning for you ... specifically, you individually.

1. Take it easy. Go slow. Proceed with caution.

   _____

2. Don't run in before you look.

   _____

3. Be careful about those that prey on the rejected.

   _____

4. Excitement isn't love. Don't get confused.

   _____

5. Don't give it your all yet!

   _____

Chapter Ten – Love of Dating
Prayer Journal

Begin by praying and thanking God for His divine love. Ask for His continued guidance, healing power and strength, especially as you head out into the world of dating. Be mindful of all your God-given abilities. Be still and listen to Him. Close your prayer in thanks and praise.

Read 1 Corinthians 13, "The Love Chapter" and note what love is and what love is not as you read through the chapter.

Now go back and read verses 4-7. Insert this phrase "I am beautiful when I am ...(trait)"

Verse   love is *patient*
Example   1. I am beautiful when I am *patient*.

List them all here, writing out the full sentence.
Verse 4

2. _____
3. _____
4. _____
5. _____

Verse 5

6. _____
7. _____
8. _____
9. _____

Verse 6

10 _____
11. _____

Verse 7

Love protects (myself), trusts (God), hopes (for the future) and perseveres (as you do all three)

Make these statements with "I" in front.
1. I protect myself,

2. _____,

3. _____, and

4. _____
   as I become beautiful (or full of love).

Read this complete sentence over aloud.

Have you ever noticed that someone "In Love" is radiant? Their eyes sparkle, their skin seems more alive, and they are always smiling. They seem to glow. Therefore, they are beautiful. That is why all bride are beautiful on their wedding day. As you regain your emotional strength, (I can do all things through Christ who strengthens me) and find yourself lovely and beautiful, you will glow with God's love because you know you are worthy of love.

Remember, God who created the universe and all living things, loves you! Could you be loved by anyone more important? As you reclaim His love for you, you will regain your emotional strength and begin to glow again with a beauty that only love can create. Do not rush into dating until you are fully emotionally equipped and ready.

Pray for the attributes of love to be found in you. I will pray for these specific traits:
1. _____,
2. _____,
3. _____.

Ask God for help on the areas that you find difficult. Put the scripture to work in your life as you come across life's situations that require for you to be "love" (beautiful).

Section Two
Love

Chapter Eleven
Love of Marriage

In the last chapter, I had you look at your *Love of Dating*. Some of you may actually hate dating, but you have a strong *Love of Marriage*. You love being married. You hate being alone. You hate making decisions. You hate being responsible for everything. On the other hand, there are some of you who are glad you are finally free. Either way, I want you to think about how you feel about marriage. Are you eager to be married again? Or do you honestly hope you never make such a big mistake again? In this chapter, I will give you some resources to study before returning to marriage, if you are one who has a *Love of Marriage*. If you don't, I still want you to follow along and read over the resources. Use the information to continue developing and strengthening yourself so that you are better equipped and prepared to give it all it takes without giving it all of you. I know that sounds odd, but consider marriage a lifetime career like parenthood. Once you are a parent no matter how old your children are, you are still a parent. As a parent, you will always love and support your child. It is the love and support that changes into age appropriate behaviors. The love and support of a one-year-old means you feed and dress the child, whereas the love and support of a 30-year-old means you listen to their complaints or problems and rejoice with their accomplishments. You wouldn't feed and dress a normal, healthy adult child of 30. So once a parent you have a permanent career title; it is the role that changes in action, even though the emotion of love never does.

Marriage is a similar permanent career. It too changes with time, but it always takes love and commitment: Love of self, love of spouse, and love of marriage; and commitment to self, commitment to spouse, and commitment to marriage. You have already read the chapter *Love of Self,* and I hope you would not marry again if you did not have love of spouse. So what is *Love of Marriage*? All three of these loves really mean an unconditional love. It is love no matter what happens. Mostly, that type of love is impossible for a human being but it doesn't mean we should not attempt it. Like parenthood, it doesn't mean you won't feel frustrated at times; it doesn't mean that you won't feel angry at other times; and it doesn't mean life is a perpetual "bed of roses." It does mean you will always approach it with an attitude of love ... love in frustration, love in anger, or love in a bed of thorns. This is due to your commitment to yourself, your spouse and your marriage. You may have been all of this before, yet your marriage ended in divorce. That does not mean that if you enter into marriage again that it is not going to take all the effort you gave before. It is going to take all that effort and maybe more. Be sure to enter into marriage with caution and be mindful that you need to approach it with this effort for it to have a chance of lasting. Emotional sleeves are rolled up all the time, and things may not seem so idyllic, but it deserves the commitment to work at it as it goes along, and not when it is too late.

You need to have a realistic view of what marriage is. You need to have a realistic conception of how much work it takes. And you need to NOT make a new marriage or spouse pay for the mistakes of the past marriage. Do not enter it with the attitude "Well, I gave it all last time, so this time the spouse is going to have to do all the work; I'm relaxing this time." It won't work that way. You are a divorcee and if you are marrying a divorcee, you will need to work. You both have come through a lot to get where you are now ... at the door of marriage again. Neither of you will want to go through the heartache that you just went through again. Sometimes, this makes persons more committed, though other times, persons actually stay distant when it comes to working at it again. It is important to know what kind of partner you have fallen for. It is important to build those communication bridges now, before marriage, and build them strong so that they will be sturdy when you use them in marriage. In movies, you have seen those flimsy, bouncy bridges that traverse a deep gorge. The handrails are made of rope, the floorboards are held together by rope, and it all droops down and sways as you walk across it. Then there are bridges that are made of concrete and have steel handrails. They are suspended over a low area that you could actually jump down into without hurting yourself. Personally, I like the concrete bridges better, and especially if it has to traverse deep gorges. Be sure your communication bridge is built strong. Building bridges takes time, and work. The finished product is worth it and saves time getting from point A to point B.

There are many more issues that you will be bringing into this marriage than you did the last time. If the last time was your first marriage, you did not have any ex and/or children immediately affecting and infecting the marriage. Ex-spouses are notorious for infecting the next marriage with poison in hopes of destroying it as well. Be aware of these behaviors. Sometimes, ex-spouses are very friendly and seem harmless, but they have no place in your marriage. Marriage is between two persons; make sure you are both clear on that before you say "I do." It is not a club of ex-marriage partners making one big family. If you end up living with the children from the previous marriage, the ex-spouse parent, may try to engage your marriage, disrupting its positive energy. Set up your parameters before marriage. Set time for the two of you. The weekend the children are with the ex-spouse may be a good time to plan activities for the two of you. Be sure to stay committed to these special activities taking place. Your marriage deserves the time, the romance, and the chance to survive. On the other hand, if you do not have the children all the time, then make the weekend you get the children all about the children and their parent. Then give the children your undivided attention; they deserve it. Plan marriage time when you don't have them. Remember, if plans change because the ex-spouse changed them, don't make the children pay for your disappointment.

All that I have been writing about is known as 'baggage.' Some baggage you can not keep from coming into the new marriage. You just need to make it as compact and neat as possible. Make it carry-on, not a steamer trunk sized baggage. A psychologist, who spoke at a separated and divorced group I attended, gave a demonstration about baggage. She went around the room and gathered shoulder bags from the women in the audience. She placed three or four over her head and neck and then she selected a man from the audience and did the same thing to him. Then she instructed him to give her a big hug. They both tried to hug each other, but the bags were in the way and the best they could do was pat their hands on the others' arms. She likened this to the marriages that we sometimes enter into without getting rid of the baggage that we have around our neck. Some of this baggage can be put down, but some can not. Do your best to remove the baggage you can put down. Select the bags that you can occassionally put down and then see if you can still hug. Give the love it takes to sustain a marriage.

Before entering into marriage, determine your role in a marriage. If you are a mother, mother your children. If you are a father, father your children. Do not expect your new spouse to do it for you or your ex-spouse. You ARE the parent, YOU be the parent. If you are not the parent, then you be the supportive spouse. Do not fall for the role of the wicked step-parent. The children will hate you and after awhile, your spouse may too.

In determining jobs (some call these "roles") within marriage, you will find people expect certain tasks to be performed, and if these tasks are not done, resentment builds when they have to perform them for the other partner.

Everyone's previous division of labor in marriage was not the same. When resentment begins to be stored up, problems begin. Even if you are not anywhere near marriage, or you are not even dating anyone, it is still a good idea to know what your expectations are. List your role expectations. List the responsibilities that you want a new spouse to have. Make a list of the division of labor the way you see it. Keep your list for the day marriage comes knocking again. This kind of clarity in communication can head off small issues before they grow into ridiculously large problems. For instance, if you think that guys take out the garbage, then make sure the male partner knows that expectation. Don't take out the garbage for a month or two, hating it in silence, and then blow-up at your new spouse because you are always having to be responsible for doing it. It is not fair to him or you. Each of you will need to communicate your expectations when it comes to the division of labor in the marriage. It is best determined before arguments begin.

Do research on marriage. Read books on subjects that can improve your skills as a marriage partner. You will want your next marriage to last and you will want to gain as much knowledge and skill as possible. Ask couples you know that seem happily married what advice they have on why their marriage is working. There are several books written on marriage. You can find others on your bookstore shelf under the section marked "Marriage." And you can also find books at your church bookstore or a Christian bookstore. You can even search the topic on Amazon books on the Internet and read over the reviews.

Before marrying again, you might consider pre-marriage counseling. If you went to a marriage counselor before the divorce, you may want to go to the same counselor with your new fiancée. The counselor will remember some of the issues that existed in the last marriage, and can discuss those subjects with you and the new fiancée. The counselor can help you with communicating what you have expressed in the past in a clear method, addressing issues that have been very important to you. A marriage counselor will know the most discussed problem issues and can address each with you. The counselor can help you both explore your feelings and views on these hot topics. I did see a workbook that was made for that very purpose. It had the engaged couple go through chapters dedicated to the most difficult issues and asked questions of each person to help the couple evaluate where they really stood on them. Unfortunately, I did not keep that title or book, but I know such work exists and can be helpful. This type of communication can be very beneficial to the new marriage.

It is important to be dedicated to being the best spouse you can be, and that starts way before the "I do." It takes more than **Love of Marriage** to make marriage survive and flourish. Use your research skills and find your own resources on the subject of marriage, marriage partners, and what makes a good marriage. The **Love of Marriage** will get you started, but it is going to take much more. It will definitely take **Tenderness**. The next section and concluding chapter is about **Tenderness**: tenderness with self, tenderness with others, and tenderness in marriage and lasting relationships.

But before going on to the next chapter, be sure to read over the case study and resource list, and use the journal and prayer journal exercises. I can't express enough times how the journal exercises are there for you to work through your thoughts and issues. They are there to help you make your thoughts and views clearer. The exercises help give you a chance to take your thoughts and views out in the light of day to see how strong or feeble they are. It lets you take their pulse, so to speak, and determine if all is healthy or if treatment is necessary. Be sure to take advantage of the journals and prayer journals.

Chapter Eleven – Love of Marriage
RESOURCES

Movies (dvd, tv, etc.)

Songs

Books/Articles/Groups/Other Resources
(and articles on the internet)

Smith, Blaine (May 15, 2006). *Pearls of Too Great a Price*, Nehemiah Notes.
Smith, Blaine (June 15, 2006). *Fooled by Fleecing*, Nehemiah Notes.
http://nehemiahministries.com

Harley, Jr., William F. (2001). *His Needs, Her Needs: Building an Affair-Proof Marriage,* Grand Rapids: Baker Book House Company. **ISBN:** 0-8007-1788-0

De Mello, Anthony (1992). *The Way to Love,* New York: Doubleday. ISBN: 0-385-24938-1

Psychiatrists, Psychotherapists, and Psychologists

Erik Erikson

Resources I found related to this chapter?
_____
_____
_____
_____
_____

NOTES

Case Study #11

Lorraine was a successful 55-year-old woman. She had been married in her younger years to a domineering husband. She had been divorced for many years. She had developed a very comfortable lifestyle as a single woman. She had established a good career, and had acquired beside regular independence, financial independence. She was debt free. She had a house, car, and investments. These were all earned by her and not given to her in a divorce settlement. She was proud of how far she had come, emotionally as well as financially.

Lorraine had many friends and acquaintances that she had developed over the years. The friends ranged from old to young. Lorraine was a very pleasant person; she was loving and giving. She was always positive and made others feel so great they wanted to stay in her presence. She participated in many varied activities with her different friends. She went on sightseeing trips with some, did church activities with others, played tennis with her sporty friends, and went to art exhibits and plays with still others.

Over the years, friends had set her up with blind dates, but nothing ever became of them in the way of romance. The blind dates just ended up being added to her list of good friends or acquaintances. Then, out of no where it happened, a friend set her up with a blind date that clicked. They found they really enjoyed each other's company, and did have many likes in common. After dating over a year, they became engaged.

Lorraine found she had many issues with trust to work on during their engagement period. One day, Ted was at Lorraine's house fixing something for her and he ended up making it worse. Lorraine knew how to fix it, but when he asked to do it she had decided to let him. She found she had to redo the job after he had left. Then another time, he ruined something very valuable of hers. He told her he would buy her a new one. She had taken all her life acquiring these things and didn't need a man coming in and ruining them for her. She was ready to call the marriage plans off. She would rather be alone the rest of her life than to have to deal with this disruption in her life.

She was about to call it all off, but something inside made her take another look for a solution to the problem. She realized she was truly in love and decided that love had to be unconditional. She decided to see him through God's eyes. She also knew that she did not value possessions more than she valued people in her life. She knew how to communicate with people. After all, she had many friends and had obviously practiced this skill often. Through expressing these feelings in good communication, they came to a win-win decision. They decided to sell off her most valuable possessions and her house and moved into his house. They wrote a prenuptial agreement regarding the money that Lorraine now had from the sale of the house and furnishings. Her funds were protected, making her feel secure in the event that the marriage did not workout or if Ted should die, since Ted had adult children who had rightful claim to his estate.

Remember, it is not easy to enter into a marriage at anytime, and moreso after living single for a long period of time. If it bothers you to have your stuff accidentally damaged, then get cheaper stuff. Don't value things too much and value the person in your life more. Realize that relationships are more important than possessions. It is not easy for women after being single and self sufficient for a long number of years to enter marriage again, even though they long for companionship and love. Some decide not to even try. Lorraine was courageous to attempt marriage in her life again. She went into it with an open heart as well as good mind.

Chapter Eleven – Love of Marriage
Journal

Read over the statements below and answer the questions that follow.

When one door closes, another one opens, or at least a window does.

Don't go for looks or wealth, go for someone who makes you smile.

Dream what you want, Go where you want, and Be what you want.

You need just enough hope to make you happy.

The happiest people you meet make the most out of everything.

You can't go forward in life until you let go of your past failures and heartaches.

1. How do you relate each of the six statements about life to your life?

    1. _____
    2. _____
    3. _____
    4. _____
    5. _____
    6. _____

2. What statement symbolizes a future relationship to you?

_____
_____
_____
_____
_____
_____
_____

3. What will you need to do first to make it happen?

_____
_____
_____
_____

4. Memories of a good life make you smile. Begin making new memories each and every day. What did you do today that you will choose to remember with a smile several years from now?

_____
_____
_____
_____
_____

5. If you did not have a notable event that you can think of, what can you plan for tomorrow or the coming weekend to create one?

_____
_____
_____
_____

Chapter Eleven – Love of Marriage
Prayer Journal

Begin by praying and thanking God for His divine love. Ask for His continued guidance, healing power and strength, especially as you continue to grow emotionally. Be mindful of all your blessings. Be still and listen to Him. Close your prayer in thanks and praise.

Read Esther 1 and 2

In Chapter 1

1. What document in our culture compares to the King's decree?

   _____

2. What grounds did the King have for the decree?

   _____

In Chapter 2

3. How did the King select a new queen?

   _____
   _____

4. What was special about the process?

   _____
   _____

5. How long did this take? Explain.

   _____
   _____

6. What tips from this chapter can you use for yourself?

_____

_____

Read the story of Ruth 1-4

7. What caused Ruth to be single?

_____

8. What did this mean for her?

_____

9. What event caused her to meet her next husband?

_____

10. Did she have spa treatments like Esther? Explain.

_____

11. Why is Ruth important in the Bible?

_____

12. Consider both the stories of Esther and Ruth. How does our culture differ when it comes to women, marriage and engagement?

_____
_____
_____
_____
_____
_____
_____

13. Find another woman in the Bible who is noted for her wise business sense. Read about her in Proverbs 31:10-31. What responsibilities does she have?

NOTES

Section Three
Tenderness

Chapter Twelve
Showing Tenderness to Yourself and Others

In the second section of the book, I had you looking at *Love: Love of You, Love of Friends, Love of Dating, and Love of Marriage.* To exercise love, you must show *Tenderness.* This chapter, *Showing Tenderness to Yourself and Others,* will have you take a look at how that is demonstrated. When you can demonstrate tenderness to your *self*, as well as others, you can assure yourself that you know what love is about and that you are ready to love again.

Tenderness is a form of unconditional and vulnerable love. Tenderness is demonstrated in the form of acceptance. You have heard the phrase "love the sinner but not the sin," meaning that you accept a person for who they are even if you do not like or condone their behavior. This is acceptance. Tenderness is also demonstrated through giving and forgiving. Tenderness is demonstrated through sharing yourself and your time in supporting the persons being loved. Tenderness is demonstrated in actions, but also in words.

First, take a look at acceptance. This acceptance begins with you. Do you accept yourself? Do you see your faults yet cut yourself some slack? Can you laugh at yourself while still working on aspects of your personality, behavior, spirituality and physicality? If you can not accept yourself, showing yourself love through tenderness, it is impossible to truly be able to do the same for others: for your children, for your friends, for your work mates, for your neighbors, and for strangers. Ask yourself the same questions in regards to others. Do you really accept your children, your friends, your work mates, your neighbors, and strangers? Do you see your children's, your friends', your work mates', your neighbors', and strangers' faults, yet cut them some slack? Can you laugh with them in love and not at them in criticism while they are still working on aspects of their personality, behaviors, spirituality and physicality? It is not always easy, but it is one aspect of showing tenderness.

Acceptance may be a form of tenderness, but it does not mean tenderness is blind and can't see flaws or behaviors that are not to be condoned or tolerated. An example of this is found with abusers and abusive relationships. Abusive behavior is not to be tolerated or condoned. There are many other behaviors that fit into this category. Remember, get professional help or suggest professional help for others and then move on. Do not be satisfied with a status quo of problematic relationships. It is definitely not a way of showing love through tenderness to do so. Actually, it is just the opposite.

Tenderness is demonstrated through giving and forgiving. Think about how a gift given with tenderness is precious and how it is to be valued like gold. When you give through forgiving, you release others from a bondage of inner torment. But just like I mentioned in the paragraph above, forgiving abuse is not staying in an abusive relationship. It is forgiving from a distance… a safe distance. It is praising them for getting professional help, but not entering back into a close intimate relationship to find out firsthand if it worked. Tenderness is demonstrated by forgiving the past and moving on to a whole and healthy life…yours and them theirs.

Forgiveness is just another form of acceptance. It agrees with the philosophy of "You're okay and I am (definitely) okay." You can show your children tenderness by forgiving their wrongs when they have shown that they have learned what the unaccepted behavior was and have corrected their behavior. It is a form of parenting with which you are probably familiar. Sometimes, you reward them for the change, especially when you know it was a difficult change, i.e. turning a failing grade into an A grade when the child is really just an average ability child, yet gave it a 110% effort. It is sometimes a good thing to actually tell them that they are forgiven. There are many ways that you show tenderness to your children. Think about how you can do the same for others: friends, neighbors, work mates, and strangers. This giving and forgiving is the form of tenderness you will want to continue to show yourself as well. Reward your heroic efforts at coming back from the emotionally devastating edge of separation and divorce. Forgive yourself if you feel you had any fault in the separation and divorce. Forgive the action without condoning the action. Pick yourself up; identify the problem areas; and make changes to reflect your acknowledgement of your mistakes. Then move on to a whole and healthy life.

Tenderness is also demonstrated through sharing yourself and your time in supporting the persons being loved. You show tenderness in supporting your truest friends through hard times: divorces, health issues, and even through difficult financial times. When it comes to supporting your truest friend through a difficult financial time, you may need to stand back. Remember, you can't just throw money at a problem and think it is going to go away. Each of us has different ways of handling finances. A friend may be crying poor mouth, saying she does not get enough child support to pay the rent, the bills, and the heat, yet she turns around and buys a hundred dollar bottle of her favorite perfume for herself. Not everyone has the same sense of priorities when it comes to finances. Why give her $100 to put toward the bills when the bills just included the bottle of perfume? You are sharing yourself and time, but that does not always mean your hard-earned money. Don't get involved in the action. That is not support, it is enabling. Support your true friend like God supports you. He watches, listens, gives suggestions, directions, and love and understanding. He shows (tells) us the truth in love, but doesn't do it for you. You have to do it for yourself, and so do they.

Take another example of a health issue. You can't do the MRI or blood test for your friend. They have to do that themselves. You can arrange to go with them. Remember, you are giving empathy not sympathy. Empathy is an understanding; sympathy is really feeling the pain. Remember to listen and love, but don't invest the total you. You can tell what you did to mentally get through it if you have experienced it. You can listen to them. You can't fix it; it is not possible because you can not physically become them. If you have experienced whatever it is that they are experiencing, then you want to show empathy, but not sympathy. Don't live it over again with them. Just be there, but conserve your energy. Your presence, your listening ear, and your love is enough and all that is really needed. When you begin living it, you do damage to you, you get too involved, you get hurt and your friend really doesn't want that to happen to you. It is often difficult to do the above suggestion. That is why so many women get so hurt over time, so emptied out of love with nothing left to give not even for themselves, because they gave more than they needed to give. Just give of your overflowing love, but not from within your cup, you need that. The hard part is giving only your excess, and when you feel the excess is gone, to remember to back off and refuel to overflowing again. Don't get close again until you do.

This is tenderness that you need to constantly continue to show to your *self*. When it is overflowing inside of you, you will be able to show it to your children, then your truest friends, and then the rest of the world. If you feel your sharing of self with others is becoming too draining, maybe you are giving more than you have to give. There is not much you can do when it comes to your children, yet there is much you can do if you feel this way regarding others in your life. You must give tenderness from your overflowing cup of love. When it stops spilling over, enabling you to give it away, then you must stop and refill before continuing to support others. This can not be emphasized too much.

Tenderness is demonstrated in actions, but it is also demonstrated in words.

Read this list over, reflecting on how tenderness is being demonstrated through these words:

- Forgive me
- Thank you
- You can count on me
- I'll be there to support you
- I miss you
- I respect you
- Maybe you're right
- Let me help you
- I understand
- You can do it, I believe in you
- I love you
- I am sorry

Maybe "I'm sorry" is an over used phrase that no longer means anything. Do you think this is true of "I love you"? Words are powerful. Some feel that if you love someone, you never have to say you're sorry because they know you love them. Do you feel that is true? What words of tenderness do you feel are important to voice aloud? If you say them, do they really mean something? If you hear them said to you, do they make a difference in your forgiveness levels?

Tenderness is a form of unconditional and vulnerable love. It is demonstrated through acceptance, through giving and forgiving, through sharing yourself and your time in supporting your loved ones, and is demonstrated in actions and in words. It has taken time, love and tenderness for you to heal after separation and divorce, but remember to give time, love, and tenderness in all you do and in all your relationships as you continue to sow seeds that you will want to reap throughout your life.

Next, you will find your final resource page, case study, journal and prayer journal. If you have skipped over all of these throughout the book, I strongly suggest you go back after reading the epilogue and complete them in order. You might have developed a small circle of friends going through divorce that you could gather in your home and meet once a month to work through the journal exercises. Over the next year of your life, you could develop a strong emotional self-esteem, helping others while you are helping yourself. Each member of the group would prepare for the monthly meeting by reading the chapter and completing the exercises ahead of time. Then, at the meeting time, you could select which questions would be ones to share with each other. As a group, you could evaluate the importance and value of the information as it related to each of you. Also, together you can encourage any member of the group who you feel really could benefit from a professional's help. If you do form this type of group, I would love to hear about the effect it has on your lives. You can email me at itsabouttime4@yahoo.com or you can contact me through the website: www.healingafterdivorce.com. This type of group and using the virtual group blog is a perfect opportunity for you to sow your seeds of tenderness through **Showing Tenderness to Yourself and Others.**

If you do not feel you could lead such a group, but want to participate in a group like that mentioned, give a copy of this book to your church leaders and see if they want to start a ministry for separated and divorced persons. Then, their leadership can conduct and facilitate the meetings at the church and maybe provide a nursery for those who have children. This would help you with your healing, as well as ministering to others that may be suffering in your church. Of course, the group would work best if once it got past the second chapter, that no one could join until the next group starts. After working through the book, the group members graduate out of this group. This way it stays a ministry for the hurting only, not a new singles group. Possibly then, you, or another person from the session, will feel led to give back. By assisting the facilitator of the next session, you allow the ministry to continue and show tenderness to others.

Now, let's move on to the final resources, case study, and journals. Roll up your sleeves one last time.

Chapter Twelve
Showing Tenderness to Yourself and Others
RESOURCES

Movies (dvd, tv, etc.)

Love Story (1971)
The Secret (2006)

Songs

Try a Little Tenderness sung by Otis Redding
www.youtube.com/watch?v=6oN7b8cRs-E
Words & Music by Harry Woods, Jimmy Campbell & Reg Connelly
also recorded by Bing Crosby, 1933 along with many others.

Books/Articles/Groups/Other Resources
(and articles on the internet)

Smith, Blaine (December 15, 2003). *Help from Behind the Scenes*, Nehemiah Notes.
http://nehemiahministries.com

All Nehemiah Notes articles since April 1997 are archived on the web site.
http://www.nehemiahministries.com/notesexp.htm#archive

Osteen, Joel (2007). *Becoming a Better You*, New York: Simon and Schuster. ISBN 0-7432-9688-5.

Berne, Eric (1964, 1992). *The Games People Play: The Basic Handbook of Transactional Analysis*, New York: Ballantine. ISBN: 0-345-41003-3

Psychiatrists, Psychotherapists, and Psychologists

Abraham Maslow

Case Study #12

Andrea was 42 years old and was recently divorced. It had been two years since the separation began and she decided to venture into the dating scene. She decided she would answer some personal ads in her local newspaper. She thought that if it seemed there was anyone there that might have something in common with her, she would contact him.

She talked with many individuals and only met one. He was very nice, but they both knew there was no real chemistry happening after two dates. They continued to talk by phone, encouraging each other in finding the right someone. Eventually, he convinced her she should try putting her own ad in the paper. He helped her write it in honest words with all the special abbreviations for the ad placement. She placed the ad and called in each day to get her calls. She was very flattered after receiving 28 responses in the first two days. She responded to five via the phone, and did meet all five. She went out to dinner with the first one. After the date, she decided she would go ahead and met the other four at a fast food place to share a soda and one hour's conversation. She was not interested in dating any of the four, even though they were all nice.

She stuck with the first one and continued to date because he showed her something she had not experienced for a very long time. It was tenderness. He did not seem interested in a sexual relationship, which was a relief to her. Each weekend, he would take her out for dinner and then she would not see him again until the next weekend. She was not interested in him physically, but she felt he was the best soul she had come across in any walk of life. She even nicknamed him Angel since she felt he had been sent by God to bring her back from the depths of depression and low self-esteem. After three year,s they parted ways and began dating other persons. The friendship taught Andrea many things. It taught her to love herself again and to take care of her inner child. It taught her to laugh at her mistakes and not to fret over them. It taught her to value her worth. She learned to explore new financial strategies and succeed in being independent. She gained wisdom and began to reach out to help others. Being taught tenderness through example gave her a firm foundation to reestablish her life.

Tenderness is a special way to express love: Love of self, Love of others. It is an unconditional love, an acceptance, and an uplifting encouragement that is not always expressed when one says, "I love you." Healing after separation and divorce takes time. It takes love, and most of all it takes tenderness. Make sure you give yourself all of these before marrying again.

Chapter Twelve
Showing Tenderness to Yourself and Others
Journal

For each of the 10 phrases below, give an example in your life when someone said the phrase to you and what it personally meant to you.

1. Forgive me.

2. Thank you.

3. You can count on me.

4. Maybe you're right.

5. I'll be there to support you.

6. I miss you.

7. I respect you.

8. Let me help you.

9. I understand.

10. You can do it, I believe in you.

11. What do these phrases have to do with tenderness?

12. How can you begin to use one of these phrases each day?

13. Do you accept yourself?

14. Do you see your faults, yet cut yourself some slack?

15. Can you laugh at yourself while still working on aspects of your personality, behavior, spirituality and physicality?

16. What aspects of your personality, behavior, spirituality and/or physicality still need work?

17. What exactly can you do about it? (Remember some things are just to be accepted either because it is okay or there is nothing to be done)

18. How can you begin to live a positive life showing tenderness to your *self* and toward others?

Chapter Twelve
Showing Tenderness To Yourself and Others
Prayer Journal

Pray asking God to use His Holy Spirit to direct your actions in ways of tenderness. Thank Him for bringing you through tough times, for restoring your soul, and giving you a new perspective on your life. Ask Him to continue to be a "light unto your path."

Don't think negative thoughts. Learn to control your thoughts. In other words, Think Positively! You have heard all these suggestions before. The first step to doing it all is to become aware that your thoughts are negative. Then, taking the thought and figuring out how it would sound in a positive statement. Finally, repeating the statement to your *self* again, again, and again. This awareness and action on your part is a deliberate action. You have to want to do it. You have to want to think positively. You have to want to change your negative thoughts. It is your free will. You know that thing that was given to mankind from the very beginning? Look again at the first sentence of this paragraph and note it is negatively stated, and that the third sentence is really the same statement formed in positive words. It seems simple, but it takes practice. Just like the football team that practices one play over and over and over until they get it so rehearsed that when the game night arrives the coach/quarterback gives the call to use the play and the team doesn't even have to think, they just do it. This is true of deliberately taking action to have positive thoughts. It must be practiced over and over in order for you to just do it. You did an exercise earlier in this book related to your self-tapes. Did you use the exercise in other parts of your thoughts each day?

Read the following passages and answer the questions, being aware how God is leading you.

1. Read the scripture verse Philippians 4:8 and note positive things in life to focus on. Then answer the following questions.

List the eight positive things to think upon. Then next to each write the opposite or negative things in life. Which do you think more about?

1. _____ - _____
2. _____ - _____
3. _____ - _____
4. _____ - _____
5. _____ - _____
6. _____ - _____
7. _____ - _____
8. _____ - _____

2. Don't focus on your past. Be grateful for the present. Think about your future. Dare to dream and focus on it positively.
Read Genesis 5:19-21 and reflect what this means for you when thinking positively about your future. What good has come out of your ordeal?

_____
_____
_____
_____
_____
_____

3. In the chapter *Showing Tenderness to Yourself and Others*, it was stated that tenderness takes giving and forgiving. Read the scripture passage Ephesians 4: 31-32. What are the negative behaviors that are listed in this scripture and what are the positive behaviors to replace them?

Negative behaviors _____
_____
_____
_____
_____

Positive behaviors _____
_____
_____
_____
_____

4. Read Romans 8:28, 31-39. How does this encourage you? What do you no longer have to fear? What are you assured of?

_____
_____
_____
_____
_____
_____
_____
_____
_____

5. Read Matthew 7:6-12, Galatians 5:22-23, and 1 Corinthians 12:4-11. Take the time to Seek God. Knock on His heart's door and have His Love open to you. Ask for spiritual strength and receive fruits and gifts of the spirit. List the gifts and fruits of the spirit below. How are these related to being positive and to showing tenderness?

_____
_____
_____
_____
_____
_____

6. What are you warned about in Matthew? Do you think that means all love and tenderness or excessive tenderness?

_____
_____
_____
_____
_____
_____

NOTES

Epilogue

Don't become discouraged. As the book is coming to an end you may feel it is taking too long, that you still don't feel you will ever be the same. The truth is you are right, you will never be the same. You are changing with every day's experiences, you are growing, you are becoming stronger, and you are becoming a new you. You may feel you have setbacks, but that is okay. It is good to recognize it for what it is and to examine it, embrace it, and then let go of it and move on.

If you find that you are dreaming about it, it may be that your subconscious thinks you haven't dealt with it enough so it wants you to hash it out in your sleep. If a dream becomes re-occurring and it is troubling you and leaving you with bothersome emotional feelings, you may want to seek out a professional to help you work out all the issues that the dream is presenting. Physically and mentally, you may have blotted out your problematic issues, but your brain will keep working on it even though you are unaware. Be patient. Keep finding self-help materials and building a strong support team of friends and seek professional help when needed.

It takes time, love and tenderness for you to heal after separation and divorce so give your *self* the time, love, and tenderness that only you deserve. Take the time to sow seeds of love and tenderness in all you do and in all your relationships and you will reap love and tenderness throughout your life refilling your cup to overflowing. You must give love and tenderness away in order to get it back. You must sow seeds to reap harvests. Sow time, love and tenderness seeds in your *SELF*, your children, your friends, your neighbors, your work mates and even the strangers that you meet. Remember God's Timing is perfect. Begin to reap your harvest with gratitude and praise.

It's About Time! It's ALL about time ... time, love, and tenderness.

Afterword

I wrote this sonnet as an assignment for English Literature class during my bachelor degree years of 1967-1971. The theme is "I don't have enough, but realized that I really have all I need." Somehow, around each 20 plus years this saved assignment resurfaces in my life, as it has just now at my conclusion of writing and editing this book. Faith is what it takes. Faith gives us hope and hope moves us forward. I have included the sonnet so that you too can realize that you have all you need to move forward. You are in my prayers.

Faith

Faith, enough of which I shall have never,
But is something I would want to store
In the depths of my heart and mind forever,
And would always pray I could have more.
For how could I expect to call on Him
And have granted the least of my wishes:
If my simple faith was like water - - thin,
And like a robbed rich man - - without riches?

For faith is the unseen which is hoped for
And the perceiving of that to be realized.
Being born with this hope I need no more;
Therefore, the mystical becomes visualized.
And so I find that faith is not obtained;
It dwells within, so how could it be gained?

About the Author

Joanne Fields Lyons earned her Masters of Education degree in Guidance and Counseling from Bowie State University in 1991. She was teaching high school full time, attending the university at night, and going through a divorce at the time. She worked as a high school Guidance Counselor for nine years before retiring. She has facilitated small support groups for those going through and recovering from separation and divorce. She maintains a web site to give virtual support to those healing after divorce. The URL is: www. healingafterdivorce. com. Currently, Joanne is available as a motivational speaker for church groups ministering to the separated and divorced. She lives in Hollywood, Florida.

About the Cover

The cover has a background picture of a field of stars indicating timelessness. Issues related to healing after divorce are timeless. The emotional pain of separation and divorce has not changed. It is the same whether it happened to someone 100 years ago or to someone last week.

The cover also pictures a pair of clock hands. The clock hands are represented in a rather ethereal way to indicate the way time passes to God. "A day is to a thousand years and a thousand years are unto a day". Healing after divorce is going to take time. The amount of time is different for each person experiencing it. And only God knows how much earthly time that may mean.

The title is more understandable after the explanation of the cover. It's ALL about time…God's time, and it is going to take time, love, and tenderness in your life. To heal the emotional pain that you feel after separation, the grief you feel for the loss of a marriage relationship, and all that encompasses will take time and effort on your part.

You can use the workbook as you work through the separation or divorce process anywhere. Working through the issues in the book can help you make the necessary decisions in your life and it is a good resource to go back to once the process has evolved. As you are reading or writing in it, no one will have any idea what you are reading unless you have told them. The size of the book gives the appearance of a college course workbook. So you can keep your privacy as you work on it during your lunch break at a fast food place or in the park on the weekend.

Made in the USA
Lexington, KY
23 April 2017